The Saint, the Surgeon
and the unsung Botanist

First publication 2014 by Footprints Press, South Africa

Second publication 2016 by Footprints Press, South Africa

website: www.hiltonbarber.co.za

Copyright © David Hilton-Barber 2016

Cover design and page layout by Anthony Cuerden
Email: ant@flyingant.co.za

Printed by Pinetown Printers (Pty) Ltd

ISBN 978-0-620-71244-6

The Saint, the Surgeon and the unsung Botanist

David Hilton-Barber

Preface

History (from Greek *historia*, meaning "inquiry, knowledge acquired by investigation") is the study of the past, specifically how it relates to humans. Herodotus was an ancient Greek historian who has been called 'The Father of History' and was the first historian known to collect his materials systematically, test their accuracy to a certain extent, and arrange them in a well-constructed and vivid narrative.

Social history was contrasted with political history, intellectual history and the history of great men. English historian G. M. Trevelyan saw it as the bridging point between economic and political history, reflecting that, "Without social history, economic history is barren and political history unintelligible. While the field has often been viewed negatively as history with the politics left out, it has also been defended as "history with the people put back in."

The historian, George Cory wrote:

It is no more than the grateful duty of a succeeding generation to revere the memory of those who bore the heat and burden of the days long gone. But better than merely holding in one's individual mind the memories of departed heroes is the placing on permanent record the account of their lives and works.

Margaret Atwood, novelist:

The past no longer belongs only to those who lived in it; the past belongs to those who claim it, and are willing to explore it and infuse it with meaning for those alive today.

History was one of my majors at university and we were lucky enough to have a brilliant professor, Winifred Maxwell, who was an inspiration. What particularly bothered her was the claim that our awareness of the past depends on our contemporary experiences. In my work I have always tried to tell the story through the words of people who were there at the time. I try to give their view, not what today's view might be; hence the importance of referring to books written during or soon after the events described.

The book is in two parts:

Part One, A tribute to some pioneers of the Cape and how they contributed to the society in which they lived.

Part Two, The account of some of my illustrious ancestors and how their lives made history in their time.

Acknowledgements

I am indebted to Francis White for access to his family records. We have spent many happy and productive hours at his historic Table Farm which, in 1811, was the headquarters of Colonel John Graham.

I am also beholden to Jeremy Lawrence for information on our common (if that is the right word) great-grandfather, Frederick York St Leger. The Internet, as ever, is a deep mine of data and the paintings of Thomas Barber are from the BBC website. The Killie Campbell archive in Durban yielded valuable material on Dr Guybon Atherstone, in particularly the three volumes of biography edited by his daughter.

My sincere gratitude is also extended to William Jevois and Fleur Way-Jones of the Albany Museum, and to Sally MacRoberts and Jennifer Kimble of the Brenthurst Library.

Plutarch: It is indeed a desirable thing to be well-descended but the glory belongs
to our ancestors.

Cicero: Not to know what happened before we were born is to remain perpetually a child.
For what is the worth of human life unless it is woven into the life of our ancestors
by the records of history?

Contents:

Preface

Acknowledgements

Part One

A tribute to some pioneers of the Cape and how they contributed to the society in which they lived.

Part Two

**The account of some of my illustrious ancestors
and how their lives made history in their time.**

1

Samuel Daniell

(Aqua tinter extraordinaire)

(1775–1811)

Samuel Daniell, an English painter of natural history, was perhaps the first European to capture the essence of the Kalahari. He arrived in the Cape in December 1799 on HMS Lancaster, 74 guns, Admiral Sir Roger Curtis in command, with six ships under convoy. This fine flotilla was to occupy the colony in the name of the King of England, bearing Sir George Yonge who was to assume responsibility as Acting Governor following the defeat of the Dutch. A passenger on the same vessel who befriended the young artist was the wife of General Francis Dundas. She became Daniell's patron and her husband replaced Sir George the following year.

Samuel was 24 years of age and even though two of his landscapes had already been accepted by the Royal Academy, he relinquished any idea of a settled, uneventful career as an artist in favour of a more adventurous life. At the Cape he soon became attached to the governor's staff and took lodging with Lady Anne Barnard, no less.

At the salon of this distinguished hostess he was to meet many important officials, including John Barrow, who was later to be knighted. Barrow had arrived in the Cape in 1797 as private secretary to Lord Macartney, governor of the newly acquired territory until ill health compelled him to resign in November 1798. Barrow was entrusted with the task of reconciling the Boer settlers and the native population and of reporting on the country in the interior. Lady Anne Barnard praised Barrow: "… one of the pleasantest, best-informed and most eager-minded men in the world about everything curious or worth attention." In correspondence with Lord Macartney she wrote: "I have had as a protégé for some time a young draftsman of the name of Daniell, one of Sir George's suite, who came out in the ship with Mrs. Dundas; he collects natural history, draws figures and animals which Mr. Barrow wishes him to annex to a second edition of his book."

Samuel later supplied illustrations to the second edition (1806) of *Barrow's Travels into the Interior of Southern Africa*, compiled from Barrow's copious notes and sketches of the countryside. (The account of his travels added much to his fame as an author and geographer)

No doubt Barrow had some influence when Dundas took over the reins of governor, for Samuel Daniell was appointed to act as secretary and draughtsman to a mission sent to visit the country of the 'Booshuanas'. The purpose of this mission was to negotiate the purchase of cattle from the tribes in the interior to replace those lost by the colonies in the Kaffir war. It was led by Dr Somerville and a Mr Truter and comprised "Seven Dutch Boors, inhabitants of the Roggeveld, together with 24 Hottentots and Bastard Hottentots, 4 slaves 20 draught oxen 18 saddle horses, and 20 large muskets". After considerable hardship they eventually reached Lataku in the upper reaches of the Kalahari, the furthest limit of any European exploration. The town founded by the Ba-Tlapi had an estimated population of 15,000.

In his book on the Daniells, Thomas Sutton records the journey:

> We can easily visualise the slow trek, with half-starved Bosjemen wandering up to the caravans in search of food; hunting expeditions taking place; the killing of a quagga, giving Daniell an opportunity of making a very accurate drawing. They soon came within sight of the Booshuana country, and were approached by four of the natives, one of whom was the brother of the king. Merry-making took place, and dancing lasted throughout the night. A long stay at the delightful banks of the Kourmann River was urgently necessary to refresh the almost exhausted cattle, and it was not before a week had elapsed that they were able to proceed.

The two commissioners went on ahead of the main party, and were hospitably received in Lataku by the King, Mooliahaben. After the usual exchange of presents, they were introduced to the royal harem and exhibited to crowds of onlookers. Here the party remained for just over a fortnight, Daniell occupying his time by drawing the inhabitants and animals, and the Boors in shooting game—their only interest. The expedition left on

12 December, not without feeling some regret at parting with so hospitable a people, and were accompanied for a long way by a large number of the natives.

At the end of their trek, Commissioner Truter wrote:

We praise God for His gracious assistance and protection through our long and dangerous journey over deserts wide and unfrequented, rivers deep and rapid, into the midst of a strange nation inhabiting a region hitherto unexplored. Our thanks are for the safe return of Samuel Daniell, who was able to record his impressions and transmit them to posterity in a manner which the written word cannot do.

Samuel returned to England in 1803 and confided to his brother:

… that when the English troops embarked great numbers of the Hottentot inhabitants were upon the shore, and expressed their concern at the English quitting the settlement, in a very pathetic manner. They dreaded the change of an English for a Dutch Government, fearing everything from their experienced inhumanity.

Samuel's brother, William Daniell R.A. (1769–1837), was an English landscape and marine painter. He accompanied his uncle, Thomas, also a landscape artist, to India, helping to produce one of the finest illustrated volumes of the period – Oriental Scenery.

In 1813 William Daniell completed what was to be his greatest artistic work, A Voyage Round Great Britain, illustrating places of interest around the whole coast. While in England, Samuel took advantage of the Royal Academy exhibitions and in 1804 showed African Animals: Pallah, Hippopotamus, Koodoo, Quahkah, Gnoo.

In his book, The Daniells: Artists and Travellers (1954) Thomas Sutton writes:

The coloured plates represent local scenery, animals singly or in groups in their natural surroundings, native types, and views of kraals. It may safely be said that never before had drawings of animals been presented so beautifully in their natural scenery. Particularly fine are the plates of the gnu, the springbok, and the hippopotamus.

It is Sutton again who provides us with a last word on one of the sketches—the famous gnu – executed by Samuel Daniell:

This is a similar drawing to that which appeared in the magnificent African Scenery, of which an amusing story has been handed down. This fine picture, the first drawn by a European artist, appeared so extraordinary to English eyes, that a General Officer, who had ordered in advance a complete copy of Daniell's work, on seeing this gnu, cancelled his order, stating that it was obvious that Mr Daniell was merely illustrating the work from his imagination.

Daniell painted animals in their natural surroundings

General Francis Dundas and his wife (painting by Sir Henry Raeburn, Arniston House Collection, Edinburgh)

Lady Anne Barnard (from the miniature in the possession of the Earl of Crawford and Balcarres)

Andrew Barnard (from a portrait by T Lawrence RA)

Sir John Barrow, 1st Baronet, by John Jackson

"Booshwanna Hut" by Samul Daniell (1804)

Lataku in the upper reaches of the Kalahari, the furthest limit of any European exploration at that time

The killing of a quagga gave Daniell the opportunity of making an accurate sketch

A particularly fine painting of a "Pallah" – impala.

Daniell's famous "gnoo"

Khoisan busy barbecuing grasshoppers Aquatint 1804

Korah-Khoikhoi dismantling their huts, preparing to move to new pastures. Aquatint 1805

Trekboer making a camp Aquatint c.1804

2

William John Burchell

(1775-1811)

William John Burchell, arguably one of the greatest of the early African explorers, was a highly talented naturalist who gathered an immense collection of plant and animal specimens including many new species. His biographer, Roger Stewart describes him "with having been the most prolific collector of botanical and zoological specimens." Burchell's accomplishments on his four-year expedition throughout the interior of southern Africa "solely for the purpose of acquiring knowledge" covered 7,000 km, mostly in an ox-wagon that he designed to serve as his home, laboratory, and library. He collected 50,000 species of plants, seeds and bulbs, 10,000 specimens of insects, animal skins, skeletons, and fish, numerous anthropological artefacts. He was a prolific artist and during his travels he created 500 meticulous and detailed drawings. His journals document the precise location, morphological features, and habitat of the specimens he collected. "While Burchell's primary interest was natural history and, in particular, botany, it may be argued that he was a polymath, who also had numerous skills. He certainly knew a lot about a lot and he could do a lot. Although Burchell had much in common with his fellow 19th-century naturalists, he was different: he was also a geographer, natural philosopher, ethnographer, draughtsman and artist, talented linguist and an accomplished author." (Roger Stewart)

In addition to natural history, Burchell made important observations in earth sciences during the expedition. He was the first person to identify asbestos in the Northern Cape and the first to describe glacial pavements (bedrock surface caused by rock fragments embedded in the base of a glacier.) He also charted his entire route, creating a "Map of the Extratropical Parts of Southern Africa" (published in the second volume of his book), which was a "milestone in the cartography of the country." In the field of astronomy he observed the variability of *Eta Carinae*'s brightness (*Eta Carinae* is a stellar system with a combined luminosity over five million times that of the Sun, the brightness of which varies significantly. In 1827 Burchell specifically noted *Eta Carinae*'s unusual brightness and was the first to suspect that it varied in brightness.) He became the first recorded person to successfully integrate indigenous herbal medicine with medicines used in Europe. Charles Darwin knew Burchell and was aware of his observations of numerous adaptations in nature.

And yet, Burchell's contributions to science have been largely overlooked. William Swainson, a fellow naturalist, collector, artist and illustrator with whom he shared numerous interests, wrote, "Science must ever regret that one whose powers of mind were so varied... was so signally neglected in his own country." In later life Burchell became a solitary and unhappy figure.

Susan Buchanan's splendid book is the source of much of the material in this chapter. The book recreates the life and journeys of this remarkable explorer.

Burchell was born in 1782, the eldest son of the successful owner of a 12-hectare nursery and botanical garden in Fulham, south-west London. The young Burchell developed a keen interest in natural history from his earliest days and was particularly taken with botany which he studied at Kew Gardens. This gave him the opportunity not only to expand his knowledge of plant life but also to meet and interact with some of the most influential natural historians of the day. Sir William Hooker in particular, the first director of the Royal Gardens in Kew, was his friend and mentor The prosperity of his father's business provided Burchell with the means to travel and his first port of call was the island of St Helena where, in the words of Charles Darwin who stopped there 30 years after Burchell, "the unique flora excites our curiosity". St Helena was then under the administration of the English East India Company and the governor, Robert Patton, appointed Burchell custodian and superintendent of the new botanic garden. Thus began his life-long practice of collecting, packaging and shipping new species of plants from different parts of the world to Kew Gardens. This was just one aspect of his life. Buchanan: "He was an active member of the community, and worked as a church warden, juror, freemason and the editor of the St Helena Gazette at various times during his stay." What was to be his heart's desire, to marry his beloved Lucia Green from Fulham, turned out to be a chimera. She was his "invaluable treasure"; and "I could never live happily in any home without my dear good Lucia." After a separation of several years, she finally sailed for St Helena to join him in 1808. However, upon arrival she announced a change of heart; she was to marry the captain of the ship that had carried her to the island, and Burchell was devastated. Her "heart was so callous to every sentiment of feeling or humanity, that she absolutely quitted St Helena with all the levity and gaiety of a girl going down a country dance." He was to remain a bachelor until his death in 1863.

In 1810, Burchell received the news that the Earl of Caledon, the first Governor of the Cape of Good Hope following its cession to the United Kingdom, "was desirous to know if I would accept the situation of 'Botanist to the Cape Colony'. (Letter from the Lutheran Minister Rev. Frederick Hesse in Cape Town, 27 January 1810.)

He left St Helena with a heavy heart having fallen out with the new governor over the management of the botanic garden but with hope for his new destination. His immediate intention was to explore the 'less frequented and unknown parts of Africa. He immediately started botanising and preparing for his journey into the interior. On 19 June 1811, he departed Cape Town 'with a mind free from prejudice' and 'solely for the purpose of acquiring knowledge'. He travelled north-east, to about 150 km north of Kuruman, to Litakun, the chief town of the Bachapins (Batlaping) where he made detailed observations of the history, architecture, population, demographics and climate. Interestingly, this was the furthest point reached by Samuel Daniell some 10 years earlier. Burchell also explored the Ky-Gariep (Vaal) River and returned to Cape Town via Graaff-Reinet, the mouth of the Great Fish River, Uitenhage, Mossel Bay and Swellendam. When he returned to Cape Town in April 1815, he had travelled approximately 7000 km, most of it on an ox-wagon he set off on a 4-year, 7000-km journey of scientific exploration.

Burchell, at the tender age of 22, had been made Fellow of the *Linnean Society of London* for, one of the youngest ever to receive this honour. This, the world's oldest active biological society, still plays a central role in the documentation of the world's flora and fauna in the interests of biodiversity conservation. It was founded in 1788, taking its name from the Swedish naturalist Carl Linnaeus (1707–1778) whose botanical, zoological and library collections have been in its keeping since 1829.)

In 1832 Burchell was made a Life Member of the *British Association for the Advancement of Science* and in 1834 Oxford University awarded him an honorary Doctor of Civil Law. Burchell's contribution to science was not acknowledged by the *Royal Society or the Geographical Society*, although he deserved the recognition.

He returned to England in 1815 with over 50,000 specimens, many of which he donated to the British Museum, Natural History (now known as the *Natural History Museum, London*). Unfortunately, many of these specimens were damaged whilst in storage at the British

Museum. This led to a dispute between Burchell and the London museum's authorities, with much resentment on both sides. Following this quarrel, the keeper of the collections named Burchell's zebra *Asinus burchelli* (*Asinus* is from the Latin, meaning ass or fool).

Burchell amassed a substantial collection on his first expedition in southern Africa; it included the type specimens of the zebra, and the white rhinoceros. Burchell set out upon his second expedition in 1825. This time he travelled in eastern Brazil, where again, he collected vast numbers of specimens including over 16,000 insects, 817 birds skins of 362 species, and many plants and other animals. In 1830, Burchell returned to Britain and in 1834 was awarded an honorary doctorate by Oxford University in recognition of his work. However, his travels had exhausted his personal fortune and he gradually became an isolated and disillusioned figure. Burchell became increasingly reclusive and protective of his collections, focusing on cataloging his vast botanical specimens but also refusing to allow others to access his collections. Some historians hypothesise that he may have suffered from a bipolar-type disorder.

In 1863, at the age of 82, after one unsuccessful suicide attempt by gunshot, he hung himself in a small outhouse in his garden. He is buried near his home in Fulham, in the family tomb at All Saints Church, Hammersmith.

Burchell's collections at the Museum In 1865, two years after his death, Miss Anna Burchell presented the bulk of her brother's entomological, ethnological, geological and zoological material to the newly open University Museum. Many of Burchell's bird and mammal types were included in this donation and survive to this day. This collection comprises specimens collected in South Africa in 1810-1815, Portugal and Tenerife in 1825 and eastern Brazil 1825-1830. His botanical specimens and manuscripts were given to the *Kew Museum*. To find out more about Burchell's specimens in the zoological collections, search under "Burchell" in the zoology online databases.

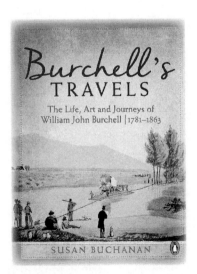

Susan Buchanan's splendid book on Burchell.

The interior of Burchell's wagon

A View in the the town of Litákun

3

Thomas Pringle

(1789–1834)

Thomas Pringle (1789–1834) is known as the father of South African poetry, the first successful English language poet and author to describe South Africa's scenery, native peoples, and living conditions. Born from a farming family in Kelso, Scotland, he was injured in an accident in infancy which was to render him a virtual cripple all his life. He attended the local grammar school before going on to study at *Edinburgh University*, where he demonstrated a remarkable talent for creative writing. This was further developed in editing several journals and newspapers while working as a clerk. In 1816 one of his poems praising the countryside near Kelso won the admiration of the novelist Sir Walter Scott. Through Scott's influence a free passage and a British Government resettlement offer of land in South Africa was secured for Thomas, his father and brother and they immigrated to Grahamstown with the 1820 Settlers.

Farming was not the young Pringle's metier and he travelled through the hinterland in search of inspiration. This is how Pringle described the Karoo in his book published in 1934 in two volumes and published by Doppler Press, *Narrative of a Residence in South Africa*.

The scenery and productions of the country reminded us, in the most forcible manner, of the imagery of the Hebrew Scriptures. The parched and thorny desert—the rugged and stony mountains—the dry beds of torrents—"the green pastures by the quiet waters—"the lions' dens"—"the mountains of leopards"—"the roes and the young harts (antelopes) that feed among the lilies"—"the coney of the rocks"—"the ostrich of the wilderness"—"the shadow of a great rock in a weary land"; these, and a thousand other objects, with the striking and appropriate descriptions which accompany them, recurred to us continually with a sense of their beauty and aptitude which we had never fully felt before. After passing the flocks of antelopes, the country became still more waste and dreary, and the noonday sun flamed fiercely down upon us from a cloudless firmament. The monotonous landscape extended round us far and wide, enlivened only now and then by a few of the larger fowls of the country; such as the white vulture, wheeling high over-head in the clear sky; the secretary bird, walking awkwardly about, with its long-feathered legs like black pantaloons, searching for its favourite prey, the snakes which infest the dry-parched land; and the stately paauw (wild peacock), a species of bustard about twice the size of a turkey, and esteemed the richest-flavoured of all the African feathered game. These, and a few ostriches in the distance, were the only living creatures we saw after we lost sight of the springboks, except the numerous lizards, green, yellow, brown, and speckled, which lay basking on almost every stone and ant-hill that dotted the sultry waste. No rain having fallen here for many months, the country was wholly parched up and desolate, and consequently deserted both by the smaller birds and by herbivorous animals. The deep melancholy silence was unbroken, save by our own voices and the sound of our horses' feet: even the hum of the wild-bee and the chirring of the grasshopper were unheard.

Pringle's literary talents are nowhere better reflected than in his poem Afar in the Desert, the last verses of which are quoted here:

Afar in the Desert I love to ride,
With the silent Bush-boy alone by my side:
When the sorrows of life the soul o'ercast,
And, sick of the Present, I cling to the Past;
When the eye is suffused with regretful tears,
From the fond recollections of former years;
And shadows of things that have long since fled
Flit over the brain, like the ghosts of the dead:
Bright visions of glory—that vanish too soon;
Day-dreams—that departed ere manhood's noon;
Attachments—by fate or by falsehood reft;
Companions of early days—lost or left;
And my Native Land—whose magical name
Thrills to the heart like electric flame;

The home of my childhood; the haunts of my prime;
All the passions and scenes of that rapturous time
When the feelings were young and the world was new,
Like the fresh bowers of Eden unfolding to view;
All—all now forsaken—forgotten—foregone!
And I—a lone exile remembered of none—
My high aims abandoned,—my good acts undone,—
Aweary of all that is under the sun,—
With that sadness of heart which no stranger may scan,
I fly to the Desert afar from man!
Afar in the Desert I love to ride,
With the silent Bush-boy alone by my side:
Away—away—in the Wilderness vast,
Where the White Man's foot hath never passed,
And the quivered Coránna or Bechuán
Hath rarely crossed with his roving clan:
A region of emptiness, howling and drear,
Which Man hath abandoned from famine and fear;
Which the snake and the lizard inhabit alone,
With the twilight bat from the yawning stone;
Where grass, nor herb, nor shrub takes root,
Save poisonous thorns that pierce the foot;
And the bitter-melon, for food and drink,
Is the pilgrim's fare by the salt lake's brink:
A region of drought, where no river glides,
Nor rippling brook with osiered sides;
Where sedgy pool, nor bubbling fount,
Nor tree, nor cloud, nor misty mount,
Appears, to refresh the aching eye:
But the barren earth, and the burning sky,
And the black horizon, round and round,
Spread—void of living sight or sound.
And here, while the night-winds round me sigh,
And the stars burn bright in the midnight sky,
As I sit apart by the desert stone,
Like Elijah at Horeb's cave alone,
'A still small voice' comes through the wild
(Like a Father consoling his fretful Child),
Which banishes bitterness, wrath, and fear,—

Saying—MAN IS DISTANT, BUT GOD IS NEAR!

He soon took up residence in Cape Town where he opened a school with fellow Scotsman John Fairbairn who he had befriended while they were both studying at the *University of Edinburgh*. Fairbairn had not graduated but apparently acquired "a passing knowledge of classical languages and mathematics". Instead he became a teacher at *Bruce's Academy* in Newcastle upon Tyne. In 1822 Pringle persuaded him to immigrate to Cape Town, holding out the prospect of a literary and teaching career in the Cape Colony. They launched *The South African Commercial Advertiser* South Africa's first independent newspaper, printed by George Greig, on 7 January 1824. Before then the only news publication that existed was the weekly Government Gazette. An article giving details of a libel suit against a Cape solicitor, William Edwards, who had accused the Governor of abuse of his powers, earned the ire of the autocratic Governor, Lord Charles Somerset. The Somerset promptly banned the newspaper and decreed that future editions would have to be submitted to censorship before printing and distribution. He also ordered Greig to deposit 10 000 Rix dollars with the Fiscal as security in case he should publish anything unacceptable. The authorities' aversion to a free press had been clearly demonstrated some years earlier by the seizure of printing equipment found on board the *"Chapman"*, an 1820 Settlers ship.

In the face of the government pressure, Pringle resigned later in 1824 and left the country to return to Britain. The New Monthly Magazine had published an anti-slavery article which he had written in South Africa before he left. This brought him to the attention of Thomas Fowell Buxton (senior) and Zachary Macaulay which led to his being appointed Secretary of the Anti-Slavery Society.

Buxton was a Member of Parliament, abolitionist and social reformer (ironically he also ran a successful brewery!) The slave trade had already been abolished as far back as 1808, but the institution of slavery still existed and Buxton helped found the *Society for the Mitigation and Gradual Abolition of Slavery* (later known as the *Anti-Slavery Society*). In the House of Commons in May 1823, Buxton who took over as leader of the abolition movement in the British House of Commons after William Wilberforce retired, introduced a resolution condemning the state of slavery as "repugnant to the principles of the British constitution and of the Christian religion", and called for its gradual abolition "throughout the British colonies". To this end he called on the government to insist that the treatment of slaves in the colonies should be improved.

Pringle began working for the *Committee of the Anti-Slavery Society* in March 1827 and continued for seven years. He encouraged Mary Prince, a former slave in the West Indies, to write her autobiography describing her experiences under slavery. This book caused a sensation and went into many editions, helped by the fact that it was the subject of several libel actions disputing its accuracy. He also published African Sketches and books of poems, such as *Ephemerides*. His efforts led to eventual success when, the British Parliament passed legislation to bring an end to slavery in the British dominions. However, the legislation did not come into effect until August 1838 and was unable to witness this moment as he had died from tuberculosis in December 1834 at the age of 45.

Back at the Cape, Fairbairn and Greig continued the struggle for press freedom. The newspaper faced further suppression and in 1827 Fairbairn travelled to London to seek justice. The Colonial Secretary gave him permission to re-open the newspaper but laid down the condition that he should steer clear of stirring up and controversy regarding politics. Fairbairn paid scant attention since he now had considerable support from his readers. Finally in 1829 the press was given absolute freedom from the Governor's control and only three decades later, in 1859, was Fairbairn rewarded for his efforts when parliament passed a bill ending any restrictions on the content of his newspaper. Fairbairn was an old-school liberal who maintained that most conflict on the frontier was entirely the fault of the colonists, not of the Xhosa, and he advocated equal treaties with the Xhosa states based on international law. He was therefore at one with the frontier policy of Andries Stockenstrom, Lieutenant Governor of British Kaffraria whose strictures against colonists from moving into Xhosa lands made him unpopular among the British settlers of the frontier. In 1851 Fairbairn, who was a strong supporter of the multi-racial Cape franchise and the emergent campaign for "Responsible Government" accompanied Stockenstrom to London in the hope of persuading Britain to introduce legislation to that effect but it was only two years later, in 1853, that representative government became a reality in the Cape. The first Prime Minister, John Molteno, hailed Fairbairn as father of representative government and freedom of the press in the Cape.

Fairbairn, who had become the sole owner of the *Commercial Advertiser* when he bought the paper from Greig, enjoyed several decades of media dominance. Things started to go downhill and in July 1853 he oversaw a merger with *The Cape Town Mail* in partnership with its owner, William Buchanan, the paper being renamed *The Commercial Advertiser and Mail*.

When Fairbairn died in 1864 the paper was taken over by John Noble, whose brother Professor Roderick Noble, served as editor but by then Saul Solomon's *Cape Argus* had made its appearance as a strong competitor. The paper finally shut down permanently in December 1879. Frederick York St Leger was now the dominant media figure with his *Cape Times* becoming the leading newspaper of the Western Cape.

Sir Walter Scott who admired Pringle's verse.

Pringle's book

Thomas Fairbairn: teacher, newspaper proprietor, politician and financier

Pringle's description of the secretary bird: "walking awkwardly about, with its long-feathered legs like black pantaloons."

The Chapman, from a lantern slide, part of the George Cory slide collection

Lord Charles Somerset, the autocratic Governor of the Cape

Thomas Buxton took over as leader of the abolition movement in the British House of Commons after William Wilberforce retired

Andries Stockenstrom; his tenure as Lieutenant-Governor was marred by virulent and libellous campaigns conducted against him

4

Andrew Geddes Bain
(1797–1864)

Andrew Geddes Bain is remembered as an honoured and greatly respected a road builder with eight major mountain roads and passes credited to him during his career. However, this occupation created an interest in geology, inspired in 1838 by a copy of *Lyell's Elements of Geology*. Sir Charles Lyell, 1st Baronet, FRS was a British lawyer and the foremost geologist of his day. Lyell was one of the first to believe that the world is older than 300 million years on the basis of its geological anomalies. He was a close friend of Charles Darwin, and contributed significantly to Darwin's thinking on the processes involved in evolution. Bain produced the first geological map of South Africa and he has often been called "the father of South African geology". His friendship with William Guybon Atherstone, who was also a keen geologist, led to collaboration in fossicking for mammal remains. Atherstone was present at the discovery of *Paranthodon africanus* at the farm Dassieklip on the Bushmans River, half-way between Grahamstown and Port Elizabeth. Bain discovered many other fossil remains, including the herbivorous mammal-like reptile *Oudenodon bainii*. This herbivorous animal, a member of the dicynodon (two dog-teeth) group, was excavated from the Karoo Beds on the farm Mildenhall south of Fort Beaufort. This was sent to Sir Richard Owen together with specimens of the so-called Blinkwater monster, *Pareiasaurus serridens*, a large quadruped, about 2.5 metres long, with elephantine legs, walking in a typically reptilian posture. Bain was born in Scotland on 11 June 1797, the only child of Alexander Bain and Jean Geddes, both of whom died when Bain was still a young boy. He was raised by an aunt who lived near Edinburgh. Here he received a classical education, but no vocational training. In 1816 he emigrated to Cape Town at the age of 19, accompanying his uncle Lieutenant Colonel William Geddes of the 83rd Regiment, who was stationed in the Cape. He married Maria Elizabeth von Backstrom on 16 November 1818 and they had three sons and seven daughters. A most versatile fellow, Andrew at one time or another was saddler, innkeeper, journalist, trader, explorer and soldier, as well as being road builder par excellence. He started his career as a saddler in Graaff Reinet in 1822 but the call of adventure soon gripped him and in 1825 he accompanied John Burner Biddulph on a trading expedition to Robert Moffat's mission station at Kuruman on the edge of the Kalahari. They explored further north and reached Dithubaruba in Bechuanaland, becoming the first recorded Europeans to return safely from so far north. In 1829 they trekked to the vicinity of present-day Kokstad. During these journeys he developed a talent for drawing and writing becoming a regular correspondent for John Fairbairn's *South African Commercial Advertiser*.

He returned to Graaff Reinet in 1834, having lost his wagons and all his trading goods as well as his collection of zoological specimens when his Griqua guides foolishly stole some cattle from Mzilikazi. This was at the time of the mfecane, a period of widespread chaos and warfare among indigenous ethnic communities when the Matabele chief ordered extensive killings and devastation to remove all opposition.

Bain was apparently outspoken and was sued for libel a number of times by Gerrit Maritz. (Details of this are scanty but Maritz was a wagon-maker at Graaff Reinet before setting off on the Great Trek as one of the Voortrekker leaders.) Fortunately for Bain the crisis on the Eastern Frontier occurred and the libel case seems to have been forgotten.

The Cape Frontier Wars in 1833–1834 dominated the area and Bain enlisted as an ensign, soon promoted to captain with the Beaufort Levies raised for the defence of the frontier. He tried his hand at farming in the newly annexed Queen Adelaide Province, but lost the farm when the land was returned to the Xhosa in 1836. Later he was engaged to construct a military road through the Ecca Pass, and his outstanding engineering talents led to permanent employment as surveyor of military roads under the *Corps of Royal Engineers* in 1836. He may well have been trained by professionals on the use of surveying instruments and the more advanced techniques of road construction but he was largely self- taught and developed his own methods from personal experience.

During this period he was involved in building the Fish River Bridge, then the largest bridge in the country, and the Queen's Road from Grahamstown to Fort Beaufort. In those days the construction of roads was largely undertaken by unskilled convict labour. An extract from *Those were South Africans* by John Bond (Page 110) reads:

> And now, with the convict gangs freed for new labours, a man stepped forward who was to become a legend on the roads of South Africa. The foxy whiskers, the intensely blue twinkling eyes, the keen humorous Scottish face and powerful shoulders of Andrew Geddes Bain, appeared at Mostert's Hoek in October 1845. It was he who would build the Great North Road to the far-off Voortrekker country.

Another description of Bain comes from a Russian, IA Goncharov, quoted in the book *Bain's Kloof Pass, Gateway to the North*, by Sandra Steytler and Hans Nieuwmeyer, Page 9 is thus:

> Bain is tall, sturdily built and strong; he walks a great deak and takes long firm strides like a an elephant; uphill or downhill, they don't change. He eats a lot like a workman and drinks even more. His face is reddish and he is bald. From learned conversation he passes easily to joking and he sings so loud that all of us in chorus could not shout him down. If he were not a civil engineer, he would be an African Rubini; he has an amazing falsetto.

1846 heralded the great age of road building and Bain was appointed Engineering Inspector by the *Cape Roads Board* in 1845. Working with Charles Mitchell (Surveyor-General) and John Montague (Colonial Secretary) he was responsible for Mitchell's Pass between the Berg River and Ceres in 1848, and Bain's Kloof Pass near Wellington in 1853. The construction of these two passes greatly improved the established route to Kimberley and the Witwatersrand. While working on these passes he also built the Gydo Pass and reconstructed the Houw Hoek Pass. He was the first man to build a road across the Limiet Mountains, the main barrier between the Cape Settlement and the interior. Grateful farmers presented him with table silver and a candelabrum for this feat. Returning to the Eastern Cape in 1854, he built numerous roads and passes including the Katberg Pass near Fort Beaufort.

The British government awarded him £200 by in 1845 for his researches. One of his most significant contributions to geological studies of the time was the first comprehensive geological map of South Africa prepared in 1852. This work was published by the *Geological Society of London* in 1856. On a visit to that city Bain was made an honorary member of the *Athenaeum Club* but his health had deteriorated and on his return to South Africa, he died in Cape Town following a heart attack on 20 October 1864.

While resident in Grahamstown he wrote some satirical sketches for local amateur dramatic entertainment and invented the character Caatje Kekelbek or *Life Among the Hottentots* (1838), also known as Kaatje Kekkelbek (Katie Gossip) who endeared herself forever to South Africans, and held John Philip and other missionaries up to ridicule.

Kaatje, the Hottentot girl, uses Hottentot-Afrikaans in the spoken parts, and sings in Afrikaans-English. She comes on stage playing a Jew's-harp:

My name is Kaatje Kekkelbek,
I come from Kat Rivier,
Daar's van water geen gebrek,
But scarce of wine and beer.
Myn A B C at Philip's school
I learnt a kleine beetje,
But left it just as great a fool
As gekke Tante Meitje.

Bain's journals were published by the *Van Riebeeck Society* in 1949. A memorial plaque was unveiled at the summit of Bain's Kloof Pass on 14 September 1953, and a memorial to him was erected at the top of the Ecca Pass on the Queen's Road on 7 September 1964.

Paranthodon, a genus of extinct stegosaurian dinosaurs

Bain became a regular correspondent for the SA Commercial Advertiser

Bridge over the Great Fish River

Bain's Kloof Pass. (Photo courtesy of Etienne du Plessis which features a horse and buggy at Dacres Pulpit, circa 1860)

5

1820 Settlers

At **this point** let us review the historical context in which the 1820 Settlers scheme was devised. Francis White, whose great-grandfather was Thomas Charles White, a prominent settler under the scheme, undertook extensive research for a privately published family history. He wrote:

> The two main streams of the European and African migrations met in the region of the Fish River in the middle of the 18th Century and in 1775 the Governor, van Plettenberg, extended the eastern boundary of the Colony to that river. The British captured the Cape for the second time in 1806 and as early as 1809 Lieut. Colonel Richard Collins was sent on a tour of investigation to the frontier as a result of serious Xhosa encroachments into the Colony. He recommended a neutral belt between the Fish and Keiskamma Rivers to keep Black and White apart. He also advocated that settlers be brought from Great Britain to increase the population of the eastern districts and that the farms should be small ones of 120 acres (50ha) each. In this way the frontier could be defended by the joint efforts of soldiers and colonists. But the British government did not encourage emigration for, since the loss of her American colonies in 1783, colonisation had not been popular in government circles. "It appeared a madness" Shelburne said "to think of colonies after what had passed in North America." Why then, the change of policy in July 1819 when the British Parliament voted £50,000 to assist organise parties to emigrate to the Cape?

Great Britain acquired the Cape purely on account of its strategic importance as a victualing station and naval base but the unrest on the eastern frontier made it necessary for her to take adequate steps to preserve the security of the Cape as a vital link in the chain of communication with the East. The only alternative to a strong, but expensive, military presence would be to settle a large European population there. So the decision to send settlers to the eastern frontier was made solely on strategic and not economic or philanthropic considerations. There were thousands of applications from the public to this offer by the government and eventually just fewer than 4000 men, women and children emigrated to the Cape in 1820. Why was there such an overwhelming response to go to a Land few of them had ever heard of? The application of steam power to the driving of machinery had led to the Industrial Revolution, which had far-reaching economic and social effects in Great Britain. There was unemployment, poverty and misery among factory workers and although peace had returned after the defeat of Napoleon at Waterloo in 1815, the country was not very far from revolution and political and economic reforms were long overdue. The plight of the poor had deteriorated from 20 years of repression and without the right to vote, they were exploited in the factories by the new capitalists and on the land by the new aristocracy. Children were working long hours in the cotton factories and the recently introduced Corn Law, designed to keep up rents and prohibiting the import of cheap foreign grain, aggravated their plight still further. And this at a time when the population was multiplying, for poverty and squalor are great breeders of children. Europe was too impoverished to buy British manufactures, and the Corn Law joined the unemployed; officers were placed on half-pay and some of the militia regiments were disbanded. The applicants to emigrate to the Cape were totally ignorant of the conditions they would encounter but on their arrival at their locations they soon realised the real motives of the British government. They were to be a "buffer" on a savage frontier between the Cape Colony and the Xhosa across the Fish River'.

The Cape, which had been occupied by the British since 1806, finally passed into her hands in terms of the The Anglo-Dutch Treaty of 1814 (also known as the Convention of London). The United Kingdom was confirmed in control of the Cape Colony at the subsequent Congress of Vienna and the connection between the Cape Colony and Britain became a permanent one. In attendance were ambassadors of European states under the chairmanship of Metternich, Foreign Minister of the Holy Roman Empire and its successor state, the Austrian Empire. Proceedings lasted from September, 1814 to June, 1815. This was the first of a series of international meetings that came to be known as the *Concert of Europe*, which was an attempt to forge a peaceful balance of power in Europe, and served as a model for later organisations such as the *League of Nations* and *United Nations*. This provided for: All powers of government within the said settlement, as well civil as military, shall be vested solely in Our Governor… All public acts… and judicial proceedings shall henceforth be done, issued and performed in the name of the Governor.

The Governor appointed to the Cape was the autocratic Lord Charles Somerset.

Ever since their arrival in 1820 the settlers had experienced years of scanty rainfall and for the first nine months of 1823 hardly any rain fell and a severe drought prevailed. Suddenly in October it rained for a week and the flood that followed destroyed their homes, damaged buildings, fences and dams, and what was left of the wheat was again attacked by the dreaded rust, this time accompanied by locusts and caterpillars. The scene was one of utter desolation. An area of 100 acres (40ha) per man was not a viable proposition especially as very little of that ground was cultivable. Lord Charles Somerset had gone back to England on leave, actually passing the Settler ships on their voyage out. Boer farmers thought that a `full farm' should be at least 6 000 acres (2 400ha) and many owned twice that much ground. Although, on their arrival in Albany the settler's needs were given every consideration by the Acting Governor, Sir Rufane Donkin, and because of his accessibility, was regarded by them as the settler's friend, things changed drastically thereafter.

On Lord Charles Somerset's return in 1821 his apparent uncaring attitude and arrogant manner soon antagonised the settlers. (He only made his first visit to them four years later). Pressure upon the authorities to do something to relieve their distress was steadily accumulating and eventually the matter was raised in the House of Commons. Early in 1823 a Commission of Enquiry was formed to examine the general administration of the government of the Cape.

Major Thomas Charles White brought out his own party in 1820, chartering the ship *Stentor* which sailed from Liverpool on 13 January and arrived in Table Bay on 19 April where the charter terminated. They were to be located at what is now known as Riviers-Sonder-End, 70 miles from Cape Town. It is not clear why this site was chosen as it was not in the remit of the Settlers scheme. In the event, Thomas White refused the location and the party was relocated to Albany and boarded the Sir George Osborne for Algoa Bay. We have a record of some interesting correspondence between the Major and the Agent for Transports, Lieut Charles Church RN. These letters were accessed from the National Archives in Kew. He had been advised of the regulations which stated that:

> The Settlers are not to be allowed to embark arms or gunpowder without an order from the Secretary of State for which it is requisite that they should apply. No dogs are to be embarked unless the parties obtain an order from the Secretary of State for the purpose, and in that case they must put on board water for them for 84 days at their own expense.

Writing from his home, Mount Pleasant in Liverpool on 20 December 1819, Thomas requested permission to take his dogs.

> I beg leave to request you will have the goodness to allow me to take 2 Greyhounds and 2 Spaniels on board the ship *Stentor*. I have not only provided Water and Provisions for the Voyage, but have also procured Crates, in which the dogs would be confined when not taking exercise by permission of the Master.

Thomas White, on half pay from the army, became one of the foremost sheep farmers in Albany. He imported special wheat seed from Paris and this helped to bring prosperity to many Albany farmers. He lost his life in the 6th Frontier War - Hintsa's War (1834 -1835) in which he served as a Major in the Grahamstown Volunteers and was employed in making a topographical survey of the native territory.

Thomas Charles White

Jeremy Bentham who campaigned for the abolition of child labour

Prince Clemens Lothar Wenzel Metternich

Rufane Donkin

The Chapman

Settlers landing at Algoa Bay (painting by Thomas Baines)

Map of the Eastern Cape at the time of the 1820 Settlers

Children forced to work in factories

"I beg leave to request you will have the goodness to allow me to take 2 Greyhounds and 2 Spaniels on board the ship Stentor."

(Thomas White)

6

William Cock

(1793–1876)

William **Cock** became known as the man who changed the course of the Kowie River and, without his pioneering efforts in the mid-19th century, the construction of the modern day Port Alfred marina development would not have been possible. Cock, an enterprising 1820 British settler had obtained approval from the Governor to improve the port (he maintained that it could be made one of the best harbours in the world) and to levy fees for goods landed or shipped there.

Originally a printer from Penryn in Cornwall, Cock led a party of 91 settlers on board the HM Weymouth, landing at Algoa Bay in May 1820. A keen businessman, he was soon actively engaged in Grahamstown in various projects. At one time he was contractor to the Government for supplying Mauritius and St Helena with salt beef, establishing a shipping line to carry the cargo. He was in partnership with the Cape Town trading firm of *Heideman, Hodgson & Co* and established a branch in Grahamstown. When he retired from this business, he accepted as his share several farms at the mouth of the Kowie River. During a visit there in 1836, Cock records:

> Whilst there I was lost to think it was much to be regretted that such a fine estuary so near to Grahamstown, and the finest county in the colony, was not made available for a port.

In 1839 he became involved in the development of Port Frances (renamed Port Alfred in 1860 during the visit of Queen Victoria's second son, Prince Alfred) which necessitated a great outlay of capital and immense personal labour. The first ship sailed up the new channel in March 1841, after which the port was regularly used by schooners plying between coastal ports.

Having been nominated by the Governor, Sir Henry Pottinger, as an MLC (Member of the Legislative Council) in 1847, Cock and fellow MLC Robert Godlonton, succeeded in getting a Bill passed for further development of the harbour. *The Kowie Harbour Improvement Company* was established and, of the £50 000 budget required (about R60 million in today's money!), half having to be raised privately. As the company's founder and chairman, and only resident director, Cock toiled for years, cutting, dredging and paving the channel, constructing breakwaters, building wharves and warehouses. All this was done with only manual and animal labour, steam-power not yet being available. Larger ships now put in frequently, the port having been declared open to vessels from every part of the world in 1855. For nearly 30 years Port Alfred was a thriving harbour but sadly Cock's enterprise came to naught when the government eventually abandoned his scheme in 1880.

William Cock was married for 64 years to Elizabeth Toy and had eleven children. He built his family a home, *Richmond House*, on the heights of the west bank, commanding a wonderful view of the river and its activities. The house was designed by his eldest son, William Frederick, not only as a residence but also to withstand siege during the Frontier wars. Its flat roof, specially strengthened to mount small cannon and fortified with battlements, led to the house becoming known as *Cock's Castle*.

William Cock's eldest granddaughter, Letitia Harriet Elizabeth Cock, at the tender age of eight, took centre stage at the renaming ceremony of Port Alfred in 1860. Here is her own account, in this extract from Reminiscences of Richmond Villa:

Prince Alfred, the Duke of Edinburgh, landed at Port Elizabeth on 6th August, 1860. He was a Cadet and it was his birthday, and he was to come to Port Frances to change the name to Port Alfred. He came as far as Grahamstown and wanted to shoot an elephant but Capt. Talton and Sir George Grey, the Governor, said he couldn't do both things - he couldn't go to Port Frances and christen it and also shoot an elephant and reach his ship in time - the "Euripides" (or "Eurius") - so Capt. Talton, Sir George Grey and staff and all the notable people belonging to the Government came to Port Frances as the guests of my grandfather. My grandmother was lying dangerously ill at the time and so she was unable to do the christening. I was the only other female by the name of Cock and so I had to christen Port Alfred. I remember two piles being driven into the river before the work commenced. Someone broke a bottle of champagne and I had to say "Port Alfred". All the staff stayed at the Castle, they had dinner there and slept there that night and next morning at breakfast they sent for me to say good-bye.

7

William Cornwallis Harris

(1807–1848)

William **Cornwallis Harris** was one of the more notable of the early Victorian travellers and his illustrations of the large African fauna were the first to have any claim to accuracy. He was not an outstanding artist, but his paintings and sketches have great charm and spirit and have considerably enriched natural history art. He hunted on a ruthless scale even as he wrote with passion about the regions he crossed, and painted the animals he encountered with great attention to detail.

Born to James Harris of Wittersham, Kent, William entered Addiscombe College at the age of fourteen. Two years later, in December 1823, he joined the East India Company as second lieutenant in Engineers, Bombay Establishment. Over the following thirteen years, Harris was posted to several places in India and was able to pursue his taste for field sports and the depiction of wildlife. He was promoted to first lieutenant in 1824 and to captain ten years later.

In June 1836 Harris arrived at Cape Town on sick leave and stayed for two years in order to recover from a fever. He was fortunate to meet Dr Andrew Smith, freshly returned from a journey north on which he had visited Mzilikazi at Mosega. Drawing on Smith's experience, Harris arranged a hunting trip to the Western Transvaal and Magaliesberg with William Richardson of the Bombay Civil Service, who had been a fellow passenger on the voyage. They sailed to Algoa Bay and made their way to Grahamstown, where they outfitted their expedition and received helpful advice from the ivory traders David Hume and Robert Schoon. He wrote:

Our purchases comprised beads, buttons, brass wire, common trinkets, cheap gewgaws, and ornaments of the baser metals, an abundant supply of snuff and tobacco. I had brought with me from India pots, kettles, and camp furniture, together with my tent, and an ample stock of gunpowder ; and a Parsee servant, named Nesserwanjee Motabhoy, who had accompanied my friend Richardson, declared his determination of following our fortunes.

Already assured of an audience with Mzilikazi, Harris thought to bring an appropriate gift.

Of dimensions suited to the figure of a portly gentleman, pointed out by the Doctor, as resembling the Chief, it was composed of drab Duffel, a coarse shaggy cloth commonly worn by the colonists, surmounted by six capes, and provided with huge bone buttons, and a ponderous brazen clasp in the shape of a crest, the whole being lined and fancifully trimmed with scarlet shalloon in a manner calculated to captivate the taste, and propitiate the esteem, of the most despotic and capricious of savages.

No expense was spared in fitting out their expedition, the equipment being readily available in Grahamstown:

water casks, tar buckets, side chests, beds, pockets, a barrel of gunpowder, six sacks of flour, two bags of rice, and two of sugar, with chests of tea and bales of coffee. The baggage waggon carried tent, camp stools, table, and cooking utensils: hams, tongues, and cheeses in profusion: salt and dried fish, biscuits, wax candles, soap, sauces and pickles. The luxury of beer, so palatable to an Anglo Indian, we were compelled to dispense with in consequence of its bulk: but we provided ourselves instead with a few dozens of brandy, and a small barrel of inferior spirits for the use of the followers. Crevices and empty spaces were filled up with spades, pickaxes, hatchets, sickles, and joiner's tools, together with nails, screws, spare bolts, and linchpins. And as if all these were not weight sufficient, no less than eighteen thousand leaden bullets duly prepared- to say nothing of a large additional supply of that precious metal in pigs, to be converted into instruments of destruction as occasion required - were added to our stock.

Harris's hunting trip from 1836 to 1837 took him across the Orange River to Kuruman. Here he met Robert Moffat who was able to provide useful information about Mzilikazi (whose abode was then in the Magaliesberg). He was also to experience at first hand the struggles of the Voortrekkers against the Matabele. Harris described Mzilikazi as follows:

> singularly cunning, wily, and suspicious, though not altogether disagreeable. His figure is rather tall, well turned and active, but leaning to corpulency. Of dignified and reserved manners, the searching quickness of his eye, the point of his questions, and the extreme caution of his replies, stamp him at once as a man capable of ruling the wild and sanguinary spirits by which he is surrounded.

The king received Harris' presents with pleasure.

> Parsee placed at his august feet the Duffel great coat which I have already described, as being lined and trimmed with scarlet shalloon; a coil of brass wire weighing fifty pounds; a mirror two feet square; two pounds of Irish blackguard snuff, and fifty pounds weight of blood red beads. Hitherto the King had considered it beneath his dignity to evince the slightest symptom of astonishment - his manner had been particularly guarded and sedate - but the sight of so many fine things at once threw his decorum off the balance, and caused him for the moment to forget what he owed to himself in the presence of so large an assembly. Putting his thumb between his teeth, and opening his eyes to their utmost limits, he grinned like a school boy at the sight of gingerbread, patting his breast, and exclaiming repeatedly, "Monanti, monanti, monanti; tanta, tanta, tanta!"

Leaving the royal kraal in high spirits, Harris and his entourage set about hunting in earnest. He shot elephant, rhinoceros, giraffe and other game in abundance. He came across his first able antelope (*Hippotragus niger*) in the Magaliesberg, and sent a description and specimen of the animal to the *Zoological Society of London*. He also sent a proposal to the geographical societies of Bombay and London that they should fund a further expedition for him to trek to Lake Ngami, but they ignored him. All the while he was sketching and painting his quarries. He made colourful observations, too, including this one:

> Of all quadrupeds, the Gnoo is probably the most awkward and grotesque. Nature doubtless formed him in one of her freaks, and it is scarcely possible to contemplate his ungainly figure without laughter. Wheeling and prancing in every direction, his shaggy and bearded head arched between his slender and muscular legs, and his long white tail streaming in the wind, this ever wary animal has at once a ferocious and ludicrous appearance. Suddenly stopping, showing an imposing front, and tossing his head in mock defiance, his wild red sinister eyes flash fire, and his snort resembling the roar of a lion, is repeated with energy and effect. Then lashing his sides with his floating tail, he plunges, bounds, kicks up his heels with a fantastic flourish, and in a moment is off at speed, making the dust fly behind him as he sweeps across the plain.

He remained at Cape Town to the end of 1837, then for the next three years he resumed his work in Western India as field engineer to the Sindh Force.

His adventures were recorded in his book, Narrative of an expedition into southern Africa, during the years 1836, and 1837, from the Cape of Good Hope, through the territories of the chief Moselekatse, to the tropic of Capricorn, with a sketch of the recent emigration of the border colonists, and a zoological appendix.

The book opens with Thomas Pringles's well-known verses from *Afar in the Desert I love to ride* without acknowledgement to the author!

His passion for hunting:

From my boyhood upwards, I have been taxed by the facetious with shooting madness, and truly a most delightful mania I have ever found it.

His early career:

I was entered at the Military College, where my worthy superiors having pronounced me competent for a commission in the Engineers, I found myself at the early age of sixteen, an officer of that istinguished Corps in Western India; one of the not least valued of my distinctions being the possession of a rifle, before the deadly grooves of which a kite had but little chance at one hundred and fifty yards.

His vision of descriptive painting:

Often in my dreams, did I see at the extremity of a long vista of years, that intervened betwixt me and my furlough, the slender and swanlike neck of the stately Giraffe, bowing distantly to our better acquaintance; Behemoth, with his square and mirth-exciting snout protruded from the yellow waters of a vast river, acting the part of master of the ceremonies; whilst a host of Rhinoceroses, supported by gigantic Elephants, eccentrically horned Antelopes, and other fascinating strangers, awaited their turn of presentation with evident impatience.

The readers he had in mind:

These pages were originally written for the perusal of some of my brother officers in India, with whom I have oft stalked the forest, and scoured the plain, and it is to them chiefly that I still present them, trusting that in the scenes described, they will recognize their friend and brother huntsman, and participate with him in the emotions which the overpowering excitement of African wild sports naturally produced in his breast.

From 1841 to 1843, Harris led a British diplomatic mission from Bombay to Sahle Selassie, Meridazmach of Shewa, at the time an autonomous district of Ethiopia, with whom they negotiated a commerce treaty. They collected extensive scientific data during the trip. Harris was gazetted major in 1843 and was knighted in England the following year for his services. After being knighted, Harris acted as executive engineer at Dharwar Dion and Poona.

During this time, he proposed a scheme for transporting shipping across the Suez desert by rail, a distance of 84 miles. The vessels would be lifted out of the water at one end of the line and put back at the other by means of a 'hydrostatic dry dock'. The rail journey would take a matter of six hours, saving two months of the voyage from India. The cost of construction could easily be recovered by a toll on shipping which would save insurance, wear and tear, and interest on money on the shortened voyage. They would 'get into the market and clear out again before vessels by the Cape could unship their cargoes.' This was set out in detail in the *Quarterly Papers on Engineering, Volume 4*, edited by John Weale in 1844.

Harris married Margaret Sligo, whose father was George Sligo of Auldhame in Scotland, and whose uncle was General Sir James Outram. The marriage was childless.

Harris died at the age of 41 near Poona as a result of fever.

"Bechuana Hunting The Lion" by William Cornwallis Harris

"Sable Antelope" by William Cornwallis Harris

"Mzilikazi" by William Cornwallis Harris

8

Dr William Guybon Atherstone

(1818–1898)

Guybon Atherstone was indeed a remarkable man. He made a profound contribution to medical science, geology and natural history, placing him firmly in the forefront of South African pioneers. He performed the first operation in South Africa under anaesthetic. He identified the first diamond discovered near Kimberley. He co-discovered the first dinosaur fossil in South Africa. He was given the freedom of London. In Grahamstown, he was the originator of the Botanical Gardens and the founder of the *Scientific and Literary Society*, later the *Albany Natural History Society* and now the *Albany Museum*. He was also an artist, a musician and an astronomer of no mean repute. He was born in Nottingham in 1818 and came out to South Africa as an infant.

His mother, in a letter to her sister-in-law, Doris Atherstone Ratcliffe, wrote: Guybon, the eldest boy, is of a delicate constitution; we therefore only give him easy pursuits, drawing and music are his favourite ones.

When he was ten he attended a course of lectures on natural history given by Dr Andrew Smith, the famous naturalist. This produced a lasting impression on his mind, and which ever afterwards underlay all his conscious life. The young fellow, who attended *Stevenson's School* at the old library in Grahamstown, always wanted to follow his father's footsteps in medicine and at the age of 15 started his medical studies under Dr Innes in Uitenhage. He was apprenticed to his father two years later and when he was 20, at the outbreak of the Second Frontier War, he acted as Staff Medical Officer under Colonel (later Sir) Harry Smith during which time he came into the possession of a valuable powder flask fashioned from the horn of a buffalo inlaid with ivory. This is a magnificent piece constructed, designed and used by the Griquas and, probably, because of its ornate design, by Adam Kok himself. It was during this trip to Bloemfontein that Sir Harry Smith said the immortal words to the Griqua's Kaptyn Adam Kok, Southey, tell them that *I am the Governor General in South Africa. If they do not leave now I will hang their black Kaptyn from a beam in this ceiling.*

When a boy, Guybon recalled riding on horseback with his father to Riebeck East where they met Piet Retief, then on his way to Natal as part of the Voortrekker movement. The object of their journey was apparently to persuade Retief to turn back from his ill-fated journey. Guybon later recorded that when the earlier Boer immigrants under the guidance of an old Albany farmer, Louis Trichardt, passed Grahamstown, the British settlers visited their encampment and presented them with a folio copy of the bible as a farewell token of their esteem and heartfelt regret at their departure.

Guybon received his certificate as a qualified medical man and was then sent by his father back to Europe to complete his medical studies. There he remained for three years, studying first in Dublin and then in London where he passed the *Royal College of Surgeons'* examination, (he was made a Fellow of the College in 1863) and finally in Heidelberg where he received a diploma at the university there. While a student at *Trinity College* in Dublin he was summoned by the House of Commons to appear before a select committee representing aborigines in British settlements which he duly did, giving his view on matters relating to the Cape. He was now joined by Fred William Barber, and together they travelled on the Continent, spending a year in Paris. Before returning to South Africa in 1839, Guybon married his cousin, Catherine Atherstone, daughter of the poet Edwin and one of three sisters renowned for their beauty. Her portrait from Thomas Barber's drawing was in the *Book of Beauty*, and many paintings of her are in existence. On arrival back in Grahamstown, he bought a house in Beaufort Street where once he and his sisters had gone to school and called it *Thursford House*, after the Norfolk home of his grandmother's family, the Guybons.

For the next 60 years, apart from a visit to Europe in 1876, Dr Atherstone devoted all his energies to the land of his adoption. He was a man with a wide variety of interests and an enormous amount of energy, and while studying medicine in Paris, he witnessed Louis Daguerre demonstrate his method of photography in which sunlight formed an image on a copper plate treated with silver iodide. Atherstone used this method himself when he a permanent returned to Grahamstown and he has left many valuable photographs of the town and surrounding areas.

He was also present when Samuel Morse, the American painter and inventor, first demonstrated his refinement of the electric telegraph and earlier telegraphic codes in 1838. He was among the first men to propose a Cape to Cairo railway, long before Cecil Rhodes.

In June 1847, Guybon performed the first operation in South Africa probably in any British Colony using sulphuric ether as an anaesthetic, only nine months after Dr John Collins Warren of Boston, one of the most renowned American surgeons of the 19th century, had introduced di-ethyl ether as an anaesthetic. Atherstone was quick to realise the potential of this new drug; his patient being Albany. Carlisle had emigrated to the Cape in his brother John's party in 1820 and at some time had lost most of the calf of one leg from a disease of the skin caused by a bacteria. Gangrene had set in and Atherstone suggested to Carlisle that he have his leg removed using this anaesthetic. Carlisle consented but stipulated that the operation only proceed when he was satisfied that the drug had produced the desired effect. The operation, on 16 June 1847 was a complete success and Dr Atherstone wrote himself into the South African history books. He was assisted by his father and two army doctors, Dr Hadway of the 91st and Dr Irwin of the 27th Regiments.

Twenty years later he was to gain renown over most of the western world for an entirely different reason. He identified the first diamond of importance discovered in the Kimberley area in 1867. The story goes that this stone, 'the Eureka', was discovered at Hopetown near the Orange River on a farm owned by Erasmus Jacobs. His wife gave the stone to their neighbour, Schalk van Niekerk, who took it to Colesberg where the acting Civil Commissioner, Lourenzo Boyes, uttered these prophetic words: *I believe it to be a diamond*. He sent the stone by mail to Dr Atherstone, who was known to be a leading mineralogist, and in due course it was confirmed to be a 21.25 carat (4.25 g) diamond.

Not everyone believed this amateur geologist living in the remote little village of Grahamstown in darkest Africa. One of the great authorities of his day, Professor James Gregory was sent out from London to make an unbiased survey of the strikes along the Orange River. He made a thorough examination of the entire stretch between Cradock, Colesberg and Hopetown and saw no indication that would warrant the assumption of the finding of diamonds or diamond-bearing deposits in any of these localities. The geological character of that part of the country renders it impossible, with the knowledge we at present possess of diamond-bearing rocks, that any could have been discovered there.

He implied that the diamonds had been salted from either Brazil or India and it seems perfectly conclusive to me that the whole story of the Cape diamonds discovery is false, and is simply one of many schemes for trying to promote the employment and expenditure of capital in searching for this precious substance in the Colony. He concluded that the whole diamond discovery in South Africa is an imposture - a bubble scheme.

Dr Atherstone was not slow in taking up the challenge and he wrote to the Geological Magazine that it should always be borne in mind that geology, like many other sciences, is not infallible, and that it is quite <u>possible</u> that diamonds may be found in rocks where past experience has taught us they never occur, but still we find the maxim *'experincia docet'* usually holds good in diamond-prospecting, as well as in that for gold. Thus was the unbiased expert from London proved so wrong by the amateur geologist in Grahamstown.

Meanwhile the Colonial Secretary, Richard Southey, who was informed of the diamond, had it sent to Cape Town where Sir Philip Wodehouse, Governor of the Cape Colony, bought it for £500 (half of which was apparently given to Mrs Jacobs). Sir Philip took it with him to the United Kingdom, where it remained for 100 years. On 16 April 1946, *the Eureka* was sold in London at a Christie's public auction as part of a bangle, for £5 700.

In 1967, De Beers purchased the diamond and donated it to the South African people. The diamond was placed in the *Kimberley Mine Museum*, where it is on display.

Atherstone's grand-daughter Ida Cartwright recorded: The story of the first South African diamond as told by Dr WG Atherstone in Grahamstown.

I was seated in my easy chair under the spreading branches of our giant pear tree in the garden of our home in Beaufort St. One sunny day towards the latter part of March, 1867, when the postman handed me a letter which on opening, I found was from Mr Lorenzo Boyes, then Clerk of the Peace at Colesberg. The envelope was just an ordinary looking one, with no seal or registration to arouse my curiosity. As I opened the envelope I subconsciously realised that something small fell out onto the lawn but took no further notice of it until, after perusing the letter I realised that what had dropped out of the envelope might be of some interest. The letter was as follows,

Colesberg, March 12th. 1867

My dear Sir,
I enclose a stone which has been handed to me by Mr John O'Reilly as having been picked up on a farm in the Hopetown district and, as he thinks it is of some value, I am sending the same to you to examine which you must please return to me.

Yours very sincerely L. Boyes

After reading this letter I realised its import, and calling to my daughter Gerty to aid me, I shouted "Come here quickly, something fell out of a letter I have just received". Together on hands and knees we scrabbled in the grass round where I had been sitting eventually recovering the pebble, a dull, rounded, apparently water-worn river stone, I had never before seen a rough diamond, but my first act was to take its specific · gravity and hardness, examining it by polarized light and so on, until I definitely decided that it was indeed a genuine diamond and of some considerable value. My next move was to hurry across my garden to my next door neighbours and old friends, Catholic Bishop Patrick Moran and the Rev Dr JC Richards, bidding them test the stone, which we did first on Ricards' sapphire ring, then he took it to the sitting room window and, on one of the panes of glass there, he triumphantly carved his initials and the date.

Henry Carter Galpin, watchmaker and jeweller of 67 Bathurst Street was also consulted. Conclusive proof was finally provided by Peter MacOwan, Principal of *Shaw College*, who determined the specific gravity of the stone which confirmed that it was in fact a diamond.

Another facet of Guybon Atherstone's widespread interests was his discovery, with Andrew Geddes Bain, of the first dinosaur fossil in South Africa, the *Stegosaur paranthodon africanus*. Dr Billy de Klerk, Curator of Earth Sciences at the *Albany Museum* in Grahamstown, published a paper on this subject in 1995 to mark the 150th anniversary of this discovery and to commemorate this event a five-metre long, life-sized reconstruction of the animal was made and is on display in the *Albany Museum*.

Dinosaurs have long held a special fascination for young and old alike. These mysterious creatures roamed the Earth for more than 150 million years before their demise 66 million years ago. Discoveries of dinosaur fossils in the early part of the 19th century in "the colonies", like South Africa and Australia, were being made but, because of a lack of expertise, the fossils were sent back to England to be described and studied by palaeontologists like Sir Richard Owen at the *British Museum* in London. It is a little known fact that the earliest discovery of dinosaur bones in South Africa were made early in 1845 by two eminent pioneers of science in the Eastern Cape, Dr William Guybon Atherstone and Mr Andrew Geddes Bain. Today Bain can, without fear of contradiction, be called the "Father of South African Geology".

De Klerk's paper recorded that Bain, "through this interest, soon made the acquaintance of the local medical practitioner Dr William Guybon Atherstone, a man whose many interests included geology and who could aptly be described as a "Victorian Gentleman of Science".'

At the close of the Sixth Frontier War in the Eastern Cape (1834-35) Bain, a settler of Scottish descent was appointed to the post of Assistant Engineer in the Royal Engineers to supervise the construction of military roads on the frontier around Grahamstown.

His first assignment in 1837 was the construction of the "Queen's Road", between Grahamstown and Fort Beaufort through the Ecca Pass. Bain developed a keen interest in the then fairly new science of geology, as his daily work brought him into close contact with rocks, minerals and fossils. He was the first person to attempt to place the rock types he encountered over the vast tracts of the Cape Colony into a geological framework.

It was early in 1845 that Atherstone, Bain, and three of his children, took a holiday excursion for the purpose of geological exploration in the Eastern Cape. At the outset Dr Atherstone did not accompany the main party from Grahamstown. He had been called away to a country patient and was only able to join them late the following day. Bain and his children had travelled from Grahamstown towards Port Elizabeth and had set up camp in the vicinity of the farm Dassieklip on the Bushman's River, about half-way between Grahamstown and Port Elizabeth. When Atherstone arrived at the camp he was greeted by Miss Jeanie Bain who was slowly staggering up the hill under some heavy load of stones. He immediately went to help her and saw that they were not stones but fossilised bones bigger than those of an ox. The discovery of these large bone fragments caused some excitement and the question of their identity and origin generated considerable discussion late into the night. From the textures of the bone Atherstone and Bain recognised that they were those of a very large reptile. What was lacking at that stage though was a diagnostic bone to give some clue as to the identity of the animal. The following day, after a long hot search, Atherstone eventually found an upper jaw bone which included a row of black serrated and fluted teeth.

At the time, Atherstone and Bain were convinced that the creature was in some way related to the Iguanodon - a dinosaur that had been discovered in 1822 by Mrs Mary Mantell in Sussex, and in 1825 described by her husband Dr Gideon Mantell. (Gideon Algernon Mantel [1790-1852] an English obstetrician, geologist and palaeontologist, was inspired by his wife's sensational discovery of a fossilised animal resembling a huge crocodile. In 1822 he was responsible for the discovery (and the eventual identification) of the first fossil teeth, and later much of the skeleton, of Iguanodon.)

Atherstone immediately coined the name *Cape Iguanodon* for the fossil and named the discovery site Iguanodon Hoek, a name which was unfortunately never formally adopted. This discovery is now accepted as having been the first record of a dinosaur find in South Africa, made only 23 years after the original discovery of Iguanodon in England.

As one can imagine, the science of palaeontology was still in its infancy at the time of this discovery and Atherstone and Bain were only making educated guesses as to the nature of the animal. They therefore resolved to send the fossil to Dr Richard Owen who was at that time the most eminent palaeontologist in England, based at the British Museum in London. It was Owen who, at a meeting in Plymouth of the *British Association for the Advancement of Science* in 1841, coined the term *Dinosauria* to describe the unusual group of large extinct reptiles that he was studying (*Dinosauria* - Greek meaning the terrible lizards).

Unfortunately only the upper jawbone and two additional skull fragments are all that remain of this find and are now housed in the *Natural History Museum* in London. No record of Athestone's bones bigger than those of an ox! has survived and it is not known if they were ever dispatched to London. It took Owen some 31 years before he published the first description of the Bushman's River fossil. Atherstone must have been frustrated at this delay, and commented on this lengthy interval in 1871 in an account of a trip which he made between Grahamstown and Port Elizabeth:

Then over the Komga [River]... Now we pass Dassieklip, where the rocks change entirely. There, to the left, lies Iguanodon- Hoek, where Bain and I years ago exhumed huge bones of some extinct Saurian - one, from the jaw and serrated teeth, I fancy some huge Iguanodon. They lie still in the vaults of the *British Museum*, unknown, unnamed, unexamined. All that is known of them you will find in the *Eastern Cape Monthly Magazine* for 1857.

The process of establishing the exact nature of the animal took a long time and a number of milestone events took place from 1845, finally culminating in the positive identification of the animal as *Paranthodon africanus (Broom)*, a plant-eating dinosaur belonging to the family of Stegosaurs. Members of this group of dinosaurs are distinct in having plates on their backs and spikes on their tails. The plates served as radiators for regulating body temperature and the spikes were used for defence. Under the auspices of the Grahamstown Prospecting Syndicate, he visited Namaqualand in 1854, and in 1870 he travelled to the Stormberg and later to the diamond mines in Kimberley and the Lydenburg goldfields.

Professor EHL Schwarz, in an address to the *South African Association for the Advancement of Science* in 1911, spoke of Atherstone as "one who was responsive to every impulse from the higher, brighter, more intellectual life, which opportunities allowed him to come across in the routine of his busy life". (Ernest Herbert Lewis Schwarz, who was appointed to the chair of geology at the *Rhodes University College*, Grahamstown in 1905, was later to achieve some recognition for his great scheme for reclaiming part of the Kalahari region and increasing the rainfall of South Africa by diverting southwards some of the head-waters of the Zambezi which he believed to have originally run in that direction, but to have undergone capture. He proposed to stop the Cunene, Okavango and Chobe Rivers hurrying the waters uselessly to the sea by damming them and diverting their flow into the Etosha Pan, and thence into South Africa for irrigation.)

On Atherstone's contribution to public affairs, the Professor referred to schemes of his, so vast and of such immense' importance to South Africa that, had they been adopted, they would have altered the whole trend of affairs, and have conferred inestimable benefits upon us. I must at the outset say that they were no mere visionary dreams - the outcome of an idle mind, but were worked for, pushed and fought for, in season and out of season, with statistics, estimates and expert knowledge.

When the Government of the Cape Colony, under Prime Minister John Charles Molteno, authorised the railway line to the diamond fields, it was laid across the barren Karoo. Atherstone pointed out how economically bad such a system was that for hundreds of miles crossed an area in which no local traffic could be expected while on the other hand, parts of the country which could support a railway along every mile of its length were left undeveloped. In the late 1850s Atherstone had already worked out a scheme for a railway through the Free State to link up all the more important centres of population.

The traffic all these years has been sufficient to pay for the reckless disregard for the future, and we are only now realising that there was some mistake in the original plan of construction, Professor Schwarz commented. The error was recognised at the time but as Atherstone pointedly exclaims, *Molteno lives in the Karoo*. Then there was the development of the Kowie as a harbour (as set out later). Atherstone strongly supported this scheme, the success of which depended, in his estimation, on the development of the surrounding districts, and to this end he tried to establish cotton growing and tea plantations, and an iron works at West Hill.

Ultimately, however, in Professor Schwarz's opinion, he intended Port Alfred to be the terminus of the Kowie-Khartoum railway. But here again Dr Atherstone was forced to realise that intrinsic merits were of no value when set against opposing vested interests, and when eventually the harbour works were commenced by Prince Alfred, who drove the first pile in 1860, the scheme was already doomed to failure.

With the economic revival of the Cape due to the discovery of diamonds, the question arose of connecting the Cape with Europe by telegraph. In 1878 the telegraph system of the Cape was joined to that of Natal with a view of eventually linking up with an east coast cable, which was actually carried out in the following year. Dr Atherstone said:

No. Why lay a cable down in the bed of the ocean where it benefits nobody, and costs an immense sum to make it sufficiently strong to resist the corroding effect of the sea-water. Why not run a line through the heart of the country to Egypt, and open up the Dark Continent to civilisation!

Professor Schwarz continues:

In 1877 Sivewright, afterwards Sir James, visited Grahamstown, and gave a lecture on telegraphy. Atherstone laid before him his plans, showing the accounts which he had at first hand from the many explorers who had set out into the interior from Grahamstown, proving that the scheme was feasible and economically possible, and he records in his notes that Sivewright was entirely convinced.

It is little known that Atherstone's great scheme for a Kimberley-Khartoum railway preceded Rhodes' Cape to Cairo dream. Had it been commenced in the 70s, it would not have faced the international complications which later prevailed and the whole course of history in SA might have been changed; in fact South Africa might then have become one province of a British Africa rather than a separate entity.

When the Lualaba was proclaimed to be a portion of the Congo, Atherstone urged the annexation of the Congo area by Britain as a necessary support for his trans-continental railway. This followed an expedition sent by the *Royal Geographical Society* in 1873 led by Vernon Cameron to locate Dr Livingstone. They met Livingstone's servants bearing the dead body of their master. Cameron continued his march and reached Ujiji, on Lake Tanganyika, in February 1874, where he found and sent to England Livingstone's papers. Cameron spent some time determining the true form of the south part of the lake, and solved the question of its outlet by the discovery of the Lualaba as the main stream of the Congo. His travels, which were published in 1877 under the title *Across Africa*, contain valuable suggestions for the opening up of the continent, including the utilisation of the great lakes as a Cape to Cairo Road connection.

Prof Schwartz concluded:

In 1875 Atherstone submitted his proposals to the Colonial Office; but although Sir William Siemens and Sir Donald Currie were prepared to back the scheme, it was not taken up by the Government. To have proved the practicability of the scheme so far back as 1875, however, was undoubtedly a preparation for its accomplishment in future years, and I claim that the Cape to Cairo railway will owe something to the Kimberley-Khartoum project.

(Charles William Siemens, originally Carl Wilhelm Siemens and later Sir William Siemens (1823– 1883) was a German-born engineer who for most of his life worked in Britain and later became a British subject.)

Atherstone recorded the events in an article entitled *How England lost Delagoa Bay* published in the *Cape Illustrated* Magazine 25 years later.

At that stage, Lydenburg was the boundary of the Dutch Republic. Atherstone, accompanied by several friends, travelled by ox-wagon beyond this boundary. He took samples and made sketches of the geological features of the area and, on ascending the mountains beyond Sabine, could clearly see the great fault in the Lacombe range near Delagoa Bay. To quote:

> I found rich visible gold everywhere. I reported the result to my friend who at once arranged with the native chief for the purchase of the whole territory for the Queen of England, the price being 15 000 head of cattle, and the chief saying he would be glad of British protection. The deed of sale was duly signed by him and witnessed, and on my return to Clip Drift I endeavoured to obtain the provisional sanction of the Government representative for six months to enable us to throw the onus of refusal on the British Government, but this was refused, the influence of the Little Englander faction was too correctly gauged, and my efforts failed.

Atherstone wrote:

> On this voyage the Portuguese Consul in Cape Town, Chevalier Du Prat, accompanied us. He was authorized by his Government in Lisbon to offer to the British Government the harbour of Delagoa Bay (where at that time England possessed only the island of Nyaka) in exchange for the duty requested me to lay this proposal before Lord Carnarvon. On my doing so Lord Carnarvon replied: "This is a most important matter. I will consult my minister and will give you a reply in a week." The reply was that the offer had been declined.

The matter was by no means dead as some 24 years hence, a certain Mr Enfield wrote a book in praise of the scheme, wherein he anticipated the acquisition of Delagoa Bay by Great Britain, which he regarded as potentially one of our most valued possessions and which will shine as one of the brightest jewels in the Crown. He went on to claim:

> It is the key to South Africa, and means much more to us than the mere acquisition of further territory, for it ensures to us our proud position as the paramount Power in South Africa, and is a most important factor in the maintenance of peace. Looking at the strained relationship that has unfortunately existed for so long past between Great Britain and the Transvaal Republic, it has become absolutely necessary to our safety that the Bay should not fall into hostile hands.

He was clearly enamoured of Rhodes who he regarded as a grand Imperialist and great Englishman. He eulogised over the magnificent possibilities of the natural harbour of

Delagoa Bay, the size, the grandeur, the natural conformation, and the unique position. Dr Atherstone's visit to England in 1875 was primarily to gather information on the treatment of mental patients for application to the Fort England asylum in Grahamstown. He was given a year's holiday by Molteno with a letter to Lord Carnarvon requesting authority for visiting the asylums of Great Britain. He was made at Fellow of the *Royal College of Surgeons* on this occasion, received the freedom of the *Turner's Company*, and of the City of London, and was admitted a Fellow of the *Geological Society*, and Honorary Corresponding Secretary of the *Royal Colonial Institute*.

In the colony, however, his services, were scantily recognised, although in 1888 the combined Kimberley companies, de Beers, Kimberley Central, Consolidated Bultfontein and Griqualand West Diamond Mining, clubbed together and presented him with a 4-carat diamond in recognition of his services. In 1881 he was elected to the Legislative Council, but the vigour of life was on the wane, and the schemes for which he had worked in his earlier years were irrevocably wrecked, and no new ones presented themselves.

In 1892 he wrote, I feel now how my life has been misspent by absence from the great centres of scientific and educational discoveries. My first practical lessons were from Faraday in science and Graves and Stokes in physiology and medicine, and afterwards by my year's residence in Paris, where I attended lectures by the most advanced scientific men of the day—French, German and American. I now feel how my life has been wasted, no one to exchange ideas with except on paper, no one to confide in for scientific research, and none to appreciate new ideas and views. Nothing but fads and conventualism - gossip and social schemes for selfish advancement and rivalry; nothing worthy of the attention except for the hour or day.

In 1890 he started to lose his sight and two years later he was completely blind but always kept an interest in all things medical and scientific. He died in 1898 and he and his wife Catherine, known as *Katie the fearless* for her courageous behaviour during the Seventh Frontier War, are buried in the Old Cemetery in Grahamstown.

Among the many tributes paid to Atherstone was one from EG Dunn, the director of the Geological Society of Victoria:

Dr Atherstone was a man brimful of original ideas, energetic to a marvelous degree, and he had the knack of imparting enthusiasm to all about him. No one excelled him in patriotic feeling; he loved South Africa and everything in it. In science he was an enthusiast; no toil was too great, task too heavy that would advance the work. Geology was his particular branch, and his observations were keen and practical.

While at the Cape in the early seventies there were few who understood the bearing of our science on economics, but Dr Atherstone fully appreciated the importance of energetically unravelling the geological problems of the country and thus assisting in its development. He was ever foremost in and out of Parliament in having such work carried out, and I owe much to him for the warm interest he took in the work during the whole fifteen years I spent in Africa, Often he had to battle against much adverse influence and the good work he did for South Africa in science when there were so few to fight on that side, entitles him to our lasting gratitude. Schwarz paid the following tribute to Atherstone in an address to the South African Association for the Advancement of Science:

In every way Dr Atherstone was fitted to enrich whatever community he chose to dwell in. That he chose Grahamstown will ever be remembered in grateful recognition, for in those days there were not many men of light and leading in South Africa, who possessed both an intimate knowledge of the country and its inhabitants, as well as a sound scientific training, and Atherstone had both. From the first he was quick to appreciate the manifold interests which this unexplored land presented to the observant eye, but I must resolutely keep in the background the purely scientific aspect of his activities— reluctantly, for I could have shown him botanising with Dr Pappe, bird-hunting with Layard, geologising with Dunn, Seeley, Rubldge and a host of others, and spending golden hours with Anthony Trollope.

(Anthony Trollope toured South Africa in 1877 and met Atherstone during his travels. His book on the history of the first Dutch and then British colonial rule, also described the people, the landscape, the sights and sounds of late 19th-century South Africa.)

Atherstonea decussata pappe is the name of a flowering plant, one of the Gentianales family distributed around the world's tropics. Dr Karl Pappe, was appointed the first Professor of Botany at the South African College in 1858). Schwartz continues:

I could have shown him also founder and often president of the *Medico-Chirurgical Society* in 1855 – afterwards the *Scientific and Literary Society* with 150 members - afterwards the *Albany Natural History Society*, now the *Albany Museum*, the same with the *South African Geologists' Association* in 1888; I could have shown him watching the infancy of the ostrich farming at Heatherton Towers and Table Farm, investigating with his father, horse-sickness and tick-fever; I could have shown him as an artist and as an accomplished musician. I want to show Dr Atherstone as one who was responsive to every impulse from the higher, brighter, more intellectual life, which opportunities allowed him to come across in the routine of his busy life.

Another legacy that Atherstone left was the Settlers Hospital in Grahamstown. He had made an appeal for the hospital as early as 1829. It was turned down by the Supreme Medical Committee:

...in view of the salubrity of the climate, the absence of dangerous contagious disease, and the small population.

The next attempt was made in 1853 by Dr Devereux, the Roman Catholic Bishop of Grahamstown. He put forward the idea, raised funds, donated land in Beaufort Street, and even started on the building; but then he died and the plan was abandoned.

Another positive step came in 1854 when the Governor made a grant of land for the purposes of a hospital. For many years funds were raised by quit-rents from this property, and when it was sold the proceeds went to the Hospital Endowment Fund. By 1857 a management committee had been formed under the chairmanship of Mr F Carlisle, the man whose leg Dr Atherstone had amputated, and a Deed of Settlement provided that 'the hospital was to be open for admission to all sick, wounded or diseased persons irrespective of colour or religious beliefs.'

Lieut. General James Jackson laid the foundation stone, and the hospital was opened on 25 September, 1858. It had cost £3,500 to build, and had twelve beds. There was a lay superintendent (Mr Mathew), two medical officers, Dr Atherstone and Dr W Edmunds, a male nurse, and five other servants. The two doctors were paid an honorarium of £25 each a year for their services. "The hospital was opened in 1858 and functioned for 64 years before being succeeded by the Settlers' Hospital".

The arms of Atherstone Priory, Or,
3 piles gules, a canton ermine

The Albany Museum - Atherstone was the founder of its predecessor,
the Medico-Chirurgical Society

He spend golden hours with Anthony Trollope

Atherstonea decussata pappe - the flowering plant namd after him

Sketch by William Howard Schröder: Brenthurst Library

Royal College of Surgeons, London, where Atherstone was later made a Fellow.

Atherstone was present when Samuel Morse, the American inventor, first demonstrated his refinement of the electric telegraph

Atherstone witnessed Louis Daguerre demonstrate his method of photography

Daguerreotype

James Gregory disputed the discovery of diamonds in the Cape

Eureka Diamond

Sir Richard Southey, sent the diamond to the Governor of the Cape

Henry Carter Galpin, watchmaker and jeweller, confirmed the stone to be a diamond

Paranthodon africanus

Dr Richard Owen, a palaeontologist at the British Museum

9

Mary Elizabeth Barber

nee Bowker (1789–1834)

Mary Elizabeth, the eighth child of Miles and Anna Maria Bowker, was born in England not long before her family sailed to the Cape as part of the 1820 Settler scheme. She was encouraged by the oldest brother, John Mitford Bowker, her senior by 18 years, to study natural sciences. She had been particularly close to her father, and had learnt from him the principles of natural history. From her earliest youth she had been fascinated by insects and plants and constantly accompanied her father and her brothers on hunting expeditions and trips around the farm, collecting beetles, butterflies and plants.

Although having no formal education apart from lessons at a farm school set up by her father for his own children and those of his workers, yet through her observation and knowledge of natural history, she developed a lifelong correspondence with Charles Darwin whom she supplied with much valuable information for the epoch-making *Origin of Species* (1859). She also materially assisted Dr William Henry Harvey in the compilation of his *Thesaurus Capensis*, published in 1859 too, many of her discoveries being named after her in this book. Mary was so enthused by it that she began a correspondence with the author which continued until his untimely death in 1866. William Harvey was the Colonial Secretary from 1835 to 1842, and a keen amateur botanist himself. He established contacts with many plant collectors throughout the colony before returning to Dublin in 1842 where he became Professor of Botany and Keeper of the Trinity College Herbarium.

As a result of Mary's connection with Harvey, she also corresponded with the directors of the Royal Botanic Gardens at Kew, first Sir William Hooker then, after his death, with his son, Joseph Dalton Hooker and his successor William Thistleton Dyer. Elizabeth sent about one thousand specimens to Harvey, which are still in the herbarium at Trinity College, Dublin, and many more to the Hookers at Kew. Mary's letters are all preserved in the archives at Kew.

It all started with a borrowed book!

In one of her earliest letters to Dr Harvey, Mary Elizabeth wrote:

> I am one of your converts: it is to you that I owe the existence of my hobby, for I never
> should have known anything of botany had I not, by mere chance, seen your
> copy of Genera of South African Plants, with the introduction to botany at the
> beginning of it. This volume I borrowed and here commenced some of the happiest
> days of my life; for in all places and at all times, in peace and war, botany has been one
> of my greatest pleasures; and often when we have been driven away from our homes,
> and have had them burned by savages, and have had nothing to shelter us but a wagon
> for months together, then botany has been my sovereign remedy to drive away care.
> And often my two little boys would say:- ' Mama, shall we ask Papa to have the wagon
> inspanned to go to another place, for there are no more new wild flowers here?' So you
> can see, anything I can do to assist you, by collecting plants, is only repaying the debt of
> gratitude I owe you for value received.

Dr Harvey, who dedicated the genus Bowkeria to Mary Elizabeth and her brother, quoted
this letter in his *Thesaurus Capensis:*

> I trust I violate no confidence in printing this lady's letter, which I do because it happily
> illustrates the power of botany to afford interesting amusement and occupation when
> shut out from society and from ordinary pursuits. How many unemployed hours of a
> forced or voluntary bush life are tediously spent, which might be pleasantly and usefully
> filled if the mind were imbued with natural history tastes! When the observing faculties
> have been once aroused and directed to natural objects and phenomena, the taste for
> recording observations and collecting specimens quickly follows, and the late victim
> of ennui now 'all eye, all ear', finds that time no longer lags, but runs only too quickly
> away. I am happy to say that I have made more than one South African "convert", but
> if my little book had produced no other result than the pleasure it has afforded to my
> excellent correspondent, and the interesting specimens she has contributed for what
> she calls "value received', I should consider myself amply repaid.

According to Alan Cohen, who authored an article in the South African Archaeological
Bulletin many years later, Mary Elizabeth deserved better recognition. He wrote:

In 1838 she borrowed a book, probably from the library of the local surgeon Dr John
Atherstone that changed her life forever. *The Genera of South African Plants, Arranged (Harvey
1838)* had just been published in Cape Town as an outline of botany for interested collectors.
It was the first substantial botanical book of its kind to be published in South Africa.

Early in 1845 Mary Elizabeth became engaged to Frederick William Barber. He was
the seventh and youngest son of the artist, Thomas Barber, of whom much later. He was
born in Nottingham , and given a good education at Eton College before furthering his
studies on the Continent where he qualified as an analytical chemist. It was during this
period that he formed a close friendship with his cousin, William Guybon Atherstone

who was then a medical student. At the conclusion of their studies, they went for a long walking tour for several months through France, Holland, Germany, Switzerland and Italy. Frederick had studied poetry at school and was delighted to visit many of the places associated with Lord Byron and was able to recite portions of Byron's poems connected with these sites. Barber decided to accompany his cousin on the latter's return to South Africa towards the end of 1939 and they sailed together on the Robert Small, arriving in Algoa Bay in December.

Thomas Barber had given his son enough money to make a start at sheep farming and to learn the basics, he started as a pupil on the farm of Dr John Atherstone, his uncle. In the ensuing five years he developed the farm, Bloemhof, which he had acquired in Graaff- Reinet, while also taking part in the various skirmishes with the Xhosas. The frontier farmers frequently met to discuss the critical situation and John Mitford Bowker, his brother-in-law to be, was often the principal speaker. Some years previously, he had been appointed Diplomatic Agent for the Fingos by the Governor, Sir Benjamin D'Urban at Fort Peddie, and was a natural spokesman for the farmers. One of the major grievances was that the Governor did nothing to prevent the sale of gunpowder to the natives.

Thus the courtship between Barber and Miss Bowker was an on-and-off affair and had been in progress for five years, before the date of their marriage was finally set. Mary Elizabeth must have been attracted to her suitor, a cultured man of many talents, but she nevertheless bore his absence with fortitude, and maintained her devotion to botany, natural history and entomology. The rest of the Bowkers had all but given up hope for a husband for Mary Elizabeth - she was already 27 - when Fred wrote to ask her to marry him. He was very busy on the farm, he said in his letter, and could she marry him in Graaff-Reinet? That was the worst form of arrogance, Anna Maria, the young lady's mother declared. If her daughter was not worth fetching, then she would remain where she was. This brought a contrite Fred down to Bathurst post haste and arrangements were made for the wedding in the Settlers' Church there. While the young couple were staying with her family at Thorn Kloof, the War of the Axe broke out and Fred joined the laager and after some weeks of fierce fighting, in which all their stock was stolen and their houses burnt down, the laager was abandoned. The men left their wives and children at Robert Bowker's farm, Craigie Burn, which was a safe haven high up in the mountains above Somerset East, and joined the burgher forces in Grahamstown for the duration of the war. Meanwhile, Mary Elizabeth gave birth to their first child, Frederick Hugh. The marriage later produced another son, Harry, and a daughter, Mary.

Fred was granted the farm Lammermoor on the Swart Kei for service in the war against Chief Kreli and it was here and later, when the family moved to the farm Highlands near Grahamstown that Mary Elizabeth made most of her botanical observations. Highlands, aptly called as it is the highest farm in Albany, described in a later book by Ivan Mitford-Barberton "in rugged country of great woods and deep valleys, in those days a veritable paradise for the sportsman and naturalist. Game was plentiful and there was much to be discovered in flora and fauna".

In 1862 Mary Elizabeth discovered entomology. Roland Trimen (1840-1916) was, according to Cohen, *'another of those young men in poor health who sought improvement in both mind and body by travelling to Africa.'* He joined the Cape Civil Service as a clerk at the age of 18. In his spare time he assisted the Curator of the South African Museum, Edgar Leopold Layard to arrange the Lepidoptera on a proper scientific basis. (Layard was the younger brother of Sir Austen Henry Layard, the excavator of Nineveh.) Trimen realised the need for a book on the butterflies of the region and in 1862 produced a small book, similar in approach to Harvey's Genera. (Layard, who later co-authored *Birds of South Africa* with Sharpe, acknowledged her letters and assistance in the compilation of their book.)

Layard introduced Trimen to James Henry Bowker, Mary's young brother, who became one of his chief sources of information and eventually co-author of a major work on South African butterflies (Trimen & Bowker 1887). Soon after the publication of Trimen's first book, Henry Bowker suggested to him that Mary might be interested in illustrating the second volume. He wrote to Trimen in July 1862:

I am trying to get my sister Mrs Barber to illustrate a copy as she can do it well and the book would be valuable. I think I told you that she painted the whole of the Albany butterflies and moths. It was a work of many years but was valuable as it were well done and mostly done upon the flowers which they loved to frequent.

Mary Elizabeth did, indeed, undertake the task. Trimen, in the preface to his book, wrote:

To Mrs FW Barber, the sister of Col Bowker, I am also greatly indebted. Long known to European botanists for her attainment and discoveries in regard to the flora of the Cape, this lady has a wide acquaintance with South African natural history generally, and in 1963 turned her attention especially to lepidoptera. With characteristic generosity, knowing I was bringing out a book on the subject - Mrs Barber offered me the fullest aid, and constantly since then have her net, pen and artistic pencil been actively engaged in the furtherance of my work. Of special value have been her graphic accounts of the habits and stations of the butterflies of the eastern districts of the Cape Colony, where she has chiefly resided, and her coloured drawings of larvae and pupae, some of which are reproduced in Plates 1 and 11 of this volume.

The *Linnean Society* published eight of her numerous monographs on South African botanical, entomological and zoological subjects as did other learned societies in Europe; some of them also being translated into foreign languages. She was elected a member of the *Hungarian Ornithological Society* and it was only through a foolish law preventing women from being members that she was not elected to the *English Natural History Society*. As an artist of no mean attainments, Mary Elizabeth greatly enhanced the value and effect of her scientific observations with drawings and painting of the objects of her study. Without any formal instruction, she produced work of professional standards - birds, reptiles, plants and moths and butterflies, a splendid collection of which is on display at the *Albany Museum* in Grahamstown which also houses her herbarium and collection of butterflies. Among the scientific papers she published were Locusts and Locust Birds, a comprehensive study of the common South African migratory locust and its predators; On the *Peculiar Colours of Animals in Relation to Habits of Life*, in which she supported Darwin's theory of female selection in many instances, the indicative colours in polygamous birds and protective colours in bright-coloured birds and butterflies, as well as recording observations on the colouring of chameleons She also presented *A plea for Insectivorous Birds* to the Eastern Province Literary and Scientific Society in Grahamstown which was later published as a pamphlet. The Journal of the Linnaean Society published two of her papers: *On the Structure and Fertilization of Leparis bowkeri,* an orchid that was named after her and her brother by Dr Harvey who compiled the *Thesaurus Capensis*, (he also named the genus *Barberetta* in her honour) and *On the Fertilisation and Dissemination of Duvernoia adhatodoites*, a plant that is pollinated by the large carpenter bees.

Two of Mary Elizabeth's papers read to the *Linnaean Society* were *On the Stone-Grasshoppers of Grahamstown*, South Africa (1869) and *On Carnivorous and Insectivorous Plants* (1870). Her best-known paper is said to be *Notes on the Peculiar Habits and Changes which take place in the Larva of Papilla nares* published by the *Transvaal Entomological Society* in 1874, which established for the first time the variable protective resemblance in the pupae of certain butterflies.

Tony Dold, Curator of the *Selmar Schonland Herbarium*, Grahamstown wrote an article on Mary Elizabeth in which he states:

Although she had an active interest in ornithology, entomology, geology, archaeology, painting, poetry and botany there is no doubt that Mrs Barber was fascinated by the stapdiads. In 1903 her memorandum to Kew Bulletin on *Stapelias* was published posthumously and the extract below is worth repeating: "In this colony the name *Stapelia* is given indiscriminately to all the different species, included in the genera *Piaranthus*, *Huernia*, and *Stapeli*. They are all commonly known as *Stapelias* throughout the land. These remarkable plants are wonderfully adapted to thrive in the uncertain climate of South Africa. It will nevertheless be found that their habits and peculiarities render them at all times somewhat uncommon and rare. A stranger unaccustomed to seek out their hidden abodes might traverse the whole country without seeing a single specimen, and yet they are so well dispersed that no locality is without especial varieties. They lie hidden in remote nooks and corners, in which they may so easily be overlooked, even when you know them well, that you will find them where you are not expecting; you come upon them as it were unawares, beneath some shady bush or perchance clinging to the face of a rugged precipice or behind some projecting rock. Some species prefer shade, while others delight in the blaze of an African sun. They are exceedingly tenacious of life, surviving long seasons of drought, and even when their roots have entirely failed, some of the succulent branches that have fallen to the earth strike root a fresh, and rise as it were from the ashes of the original plant. *Stapelias* are true evolutionists, they do not grow where they would choose to grow, nor where they would thrive the best, but where they are enabled to hold their own against an all-powerful and overwhelming host of grasses, and other irrepressible plants, in some secluded spot, frequently where a shelving rock will lend a helping hand against invasion. Nevertheless I am sorry to state that these interesting plants are rapidly disappearing from all parts of South Africa. Civilisation and colonisation, are both dead against them. They are eaten up by 'all kinds and conditions' of cattle. For instance, if an ostrich finds a *Stapelia* plant he seldom leaves without taking nearly the whole of it with him. Cattle, sheep and goats, in like manner feed upon them greedily. The native tribes during years of severe drought and famine use these plants as food, and native children delight in their sweet young succulent branches.

The florist and the gardener go hand in hand with the rest of this work of destruction, for you will hear them exclaiming 'Oh! Here is one of those curious Stapelias,' and it will be speedily pulled up and planted in some flowerbed, where for want of care it will be over-grown by other plants and lost. As a rule *Stapelias* do not seed freely; a great proportion of the flowers remain unfertilised. When fertilisation has taken place the large blossom speedily falls, while the stem with the ovary grows thick and large, and turns down where it becomes hidden among the succulent branches, remaining in this position during the whole of the ensuing winter; being thus secure from all harm, not rising again until after the rains have fallen in spring, at which time it will be observed mounting up in a perpendicular manner from its lowly bed, and standing out above the plant, when the main pods will be rapidly developed like great horns. They then remain stationary until they become ripe, when the pods open and the winged seeds are carried off by the first high wind that blows and removed far from the locality and the lowly plant from whence they sprang, and the world is all before them.'

Dold goes on: Cohen (2000) has established that approximately 1 000 carefully preserved specimens were sent to Harvey over the years and that Mrs Barber is credited with having discovered at least two new species of *Stapelia S glabricaulis*. A set of 68 of her water colours were donated to the *Albany Museum* by her family include 11 birds with their nests and eggs, two reptiles (a snake and a chameleon), 22 butterflies and 26 plants, 20 of which are *Stapeliads*. The remaining 7 are scenes of Kimberley around 1871, at the time of the diamond rush.

Although she was without any formal instruction; in drawing or painting, Schonland (1904) commented, Many of the samples of her brush could scarcely be surpassed by a good professional artist.

Unfortunately many of these paintings were destroyed by fire in 1942 but 10 of the *Stepeliads* are mounted in the *Schonland Herbarium*. The original paintings measure about 25cm x 30cm and are on grey-coloured, fairly coarse-grained paper.

Mary Elizabeth's wide-ranging interests soon extended into geology and prehistory, again sparked by her brother, Frederick William, who brought to bear his knowledge of analytical chemistry. At that time the scientific community in the Eastern Province centred on a few people such as the Atherstone family and Andrew Geddes Bain. Their collection of fossils was exhibited in Grahamstown before being sent to the Geological Society in London in 1844, thus attracting the attention of prominent geologists and palaeontologists. Frederick William wrote to his brother Henry in New York in that year: A few gentlemen have lately turned their attention to geology of the Frontier - several certain fossil remains have lately been found hitherto undescribed - and have been sent to the Geological Society in London and we are anxiously awaiting to hear the result.

Several new minerals have been found. But we sadly want an experienced hand to set us on the right track. We have neither chemists, mineralogists or geologists to direct us - I have hitherto not been able to send home for books, apparatus or chemical substances but I am sending now for some.

Mary's early years in 'geologising' - as she put it - were further encouraged by her eldest brother Mitford. While he was in charge of a burger volunteer unit during the Seventh Frontier War of 1846-7 he made time to go "poking about amongst the rocks". He wrote to his sister:

... my discoveries here lie like your own in the Pleistocene (sic) formations. The drip calk in this kloof is a conglomerate of sticks, leaves, seeds, flags etc., all beautifully perfect, the leaves having their finest fibrous veins quite perfect so you can see to what trees they belong. I should suspect your bones (referring to Mary's collection of fossils) belonging to recent animals - sea cows, hartebeests etc. Save specimens if you can.

In her reply, Mary described her findings of fossils in the area around the farm Portlock near Graaff-Reinet.

We have found a good many fossil bones up here, but they are very much broken and the rocks that they are in are mortal hard. Fred found a pretty piece of a fossil fish with the colour of the scales beautifully preserved, and they say that there is a large bed of fossil shells up in the Sneeubergen...

Mary retained her interest in fossils throughout her life though she could have made her name more famous in 1878. In a letter to Trimen in that year she wrote that she and her daughter Highlie were bathing that morning in the Vaal River they found:

...upon the slaty rocks that were cropping out into the river the footprint of one of the creatures of "the days that are no more". It might have been the impression of a bird's foot, two of the toes were quite perfect, the third was only partly visible owing to the rock having crumbled away by the wear and tear of atmospheric influences, this footprint greatly resembled some of those which Charles Lyell pictured in his introduction to geology.

The book she refers to was Sir Charles Lyell's *The Elements of Geology* (1865) which described fossil footprints found in the United States in 1842, as well as in England some years later. Most of these were from creatures with four or five toes, although he did mention the discovery of bird-like prints from a creature apparently four times larger than an ostrich. Mary Elizabeth's discovery was very likely one of the earliest findings of a bird-footed dinosaur, but the knowledge of such a creature was not available at that time. It was not until 1922 that it was finally realised that this was the first true dinosaur fossil to be found in South Africa - a stegosaur, now known as *Paranthodon africanus* (De Klerk et al. 1922).

Mary and her brother Thomas Holden Bowker were probably the first people in South Africa to recognise the existence of prehistoric stone implements in the Cape. Bowker was better known as Commandant of Burger forces during the Frontier Wars. In the War of 1850-53 he famously defended the small township of Whittlesea (named after the birthplace of Sir Harry Smith) against the Xhosas. He also founded the settlement which became known as Queenstown, using a hexagonal defence system which he designed but which came to be known as the Cathcart system after the then Governor of the Cape Colony, Sir George Cathcart, who was a great friend of Holden's. He served for many years in the Cape Legislature and in 1863 was nominated for Presidency of the Orange Free State. However he was outvoted by Jan Brand who became the new president.

According to the historian, Harold Edward Hockley (The Story of the British Settlers of 1820 in South Africa) had this unique woman had the benefit of a thorough European education her contribution to science would still be recognised as outstanding; when we reflect that from the age of two years practically her whole life was spent on the frontier, sharing in all the hardships and dangers of her menfolk and assisting them in four Kaffir Wars, and that she revisited Europe only once - seven years before her death, and long after her life's work was complete - her accomplishments and output can only be regarded as phenomenal.

The Bowker family's legacy is hardly recognised. In their time when most intellectuals and scientists could still not bring themselves to oppose the church's teachings that the time frame given in the Book of Genesis for Creation was the word of God. The discovery of stone tools in proximity to the remains of extinct mammals led the British Association for the Advancement of Science to conclude that mankind had existed at the same time as extinct mammals. This was further corroborated by the discoveries at Abbeville in northern France. However, in a remote corner of the Dark Continent a relatively unknown family of sheep farmers which had emigrated from England in 1820 and settled near Grahamstown, had anticipated their findings by at least a year. In 1870 Mary accompanied her husband to the diamond fields of Griqualand West, living for years in wagons and tents, all her spare time being occupied in the continuance of her studies and in making collections. Her home was the rendezvous of many men of note who visited the country during the early days. In

1880 she went to live with her sons at 'Junction Drift', a farm on the Great Fish River, and in 1886, when gold was discovered on the Witwatersrand, she accompanied them there.

In 1889 Mary visited Europe for the first time since her childhood. She travelled widely in England and on the Continent and returned in 1892. She visited the Cape Colony at various times and often stayed in Natal with her brother, James Henry Bowker.

During her lifetime, she presented to the Albany Museum in Grahamstown her herbarium and her collection of butterflies, and her children followed this example by presenting her paintings to the same institution. And she was gifted in music and poetry, a collection of 50 of her poems being published, "The Erythrina Tree and Other Verses" a year before her death in Malvern, Natal Province on 4 September 1899.

This poem on the Erythrina tree or Kaffir-boom is quoted from Mary's book of verse.

Bright, glorious Erythrina tree,
Queen of the forests near the sea,
Herald of springtide, wild and free.
Thy scarlet blossoms reared on high,
Above the woods in beauty lie,
Tinted in russet purple dye;
While morning beams in laughing glances
are quivering amongst thy branches
And glowing flowers as day advances.

Bright, glorious Erythrina tree,
Queen of the woodlands near the sea,
Haunt of the sun-bird and the bee.
'Neath sunny skies they feast for hours,
Quaffing the nectar of the flowers
Whose scarlet petals fall in showers.
On dark and amethystine wing,
Flitting from flow'r to flow'r they sing
Their joyous songs to thee in Spring.
A shower of ringing notes on high,
Apparently from out the sky,
Descend on earth all merrily;
While the cicada's ceaseless strain
From day to day— again, again,
Is heard through forest, dell and lane
Thrilling the woods, a wild refrain

Frederick William Barber

Anna Maria Bowker

Roland Trimen acknowledged her assistance in
the compilation of his book on butterflies

African Hoepoe

Charles Lyell's book on geology inspired her
fossil-finding exploits

Thomas Holden and Julia Bowker

Mary Eizabeth was in lifelong correspondence
with Charles Darwin

She assisted Dr William Henry Harvey in the compilation of
his Thesaurus Capensis

10

The Frontier Wars

(1789–1834)

The series of clashes historically known as the Frontier Wars date back to 1779 when Xhosa, Boer, Khoikhoi, San and the British clashed intermittently for nearly a hundred years. This was largely due to colonial expansion which in turn dispossessed Xhosa and Khoikhoi people of their land and cattle among other things. Although periods between the wars were relatively calm, there were incidents of minor skirmishes sparked by stock theft. In addition, alleged violations of signed or verbal agreements played a vital role in sparking the incidents of armed confrontations. Colonists also sought to consolidate their gains through the presence of military force as witnessed in the building of forts, garrisons, military posts and signal towers. Resistance from particularly the Xhosa was a cohesive one; other Xhosa ethnic groups cooperated with the colonial government when they felt doing so would advance their own interests.

During the early years before Dutch occupation of the region, the Xhosa, Khoikhoi and San focused primarily on hunting, agriculture and stock farming. In the 1700's the lack of sufficient space for proper stock farming forced the farmers to pack their possessions into their ox wagons and move deeper into the interior of the Cape Colony. These farmers were called 'Trek boers'. Until 1750 (29 years before the First Frontier War), migrant farmers advanced rapidly into the interior using force. For instance, the use of superior weapons such as guns quickly subdued resistance from local people. Those people who were subdued and those submitted to Trek Boers as an attempt to protect their livestock and land were employed to tend to the cattle and provide other labour needs of the white farmers. However, the Dutch East India Company (VOC) became worried about the migrant farmers moving so far because it became increasingly difficult to exercise any authority over them. In order to maintain its authority, the VOC was forced to follow in their tracks. This constant moving also resulted in the VOC having to continually change the boundaries of the eastern part of the Cape Colony. Eventually, in 1778 less than a year into the First Frontier War, the Great Fish River became the eastern frontier. It was also here that the migrant farmers first experienced problems with the Xhosa.

Until that time, the migrant farmers had only experienced serious clashes with the San people when the San attacked them with poisoned arrows and hunted their cattle. The migrant farmers frequently organised hunting parties in reprisal for the San attacks. When the frontier farmers, as they were now called, met with the Xhosa, serious clashes broke out. Each group felt that the other was intruding on their territory and disrupting their livelihood, and both wanted to protect themselves at all costs.

The VOC. established new districts such as Swellendam and Graaff-Reinet in order to maintain authority over the frontier and to quell the ongoing violence, but to no avail. The frontier farmers kept on moving across the border and the Xhosa vigorously resisted this incursion. A number of wars followed as both groups fought each other over territory and resources.

The historian Theal recalls that what was termed the Seventh Frontier War resulted from the theft of an axe at Fort Beaufort in March 1846. The suspect, handcuffed to a Hottentot prisoner, was sent to Grahamstown for trial. On the way, he was rescued by a group of his tribesmen who were obliged to cut off the Hottentot's hand in order to free their kinsman.

A military force was immediately despatched to confront the Ngqika chief, Mgolombane Sandile, but was temporarily delayed at the Amatola Mountains and the attacking Xhosas were able to ambush the patrol and capture the three mile long wagon train which was not being defended, carrying away the British officer's supply of wine and other supplies. The British not only suffered the loss of many men killed and wounded, but also the indignity of losing 61 wagons laden with baggage and stores. The column fought its way back to the mission station at Lovedale where a large stone building was converted to a temporary fort. As Theal puts it:

> And now the terrible scene was again witnessed of a great barbarian horde rushing into the colony, murdering, plundering and devastating far and wide. Once more hundreds of British and Dutch families were reduced from comfort to destitution, and were thrown upon the Government for support in the towns and lagers to which they barely escaped with their lives.

A considerable force was sent to restore order and for the first time, the Buffalo River was used for landing troops and stores. Fort Glamorgan was built on the right bank and garrisoned and a small village named East London was created there. (In later years this was converted to a prison. Our daughter, Bridget, while a student at Rhodes University in Grahamstown, spent part of her 90 days detention in there in 1986. Her offence? She was a member of the End Conscription Campaign which sought to halt compulsory military service for whites at a time when the Defence Force, when it was not involved in military action in Angola, was used in patrolling the black townships.)

Chief Mgolombane Sandile, Chief of the Ngqika (Gaikas) and his family

Cape Mounted Rifles chasing enemy

Trek Boer's way of life

11

Thomas Bain

(1830–1893)

I f there is one splendid example of a son following in his father's footsteps, look no further than Thomas Bain. These two pioneers in the technology of road engineering left a legacy which endures until today.

He was born on 20 September 1830 in Graaff Reinet, the seventh child and second son of Andrew Geddes Bain and Maria von Backström (the daughter of Johann Georg Friedrich von Backstrom from Germany). Being highly-educated themselves, his parents placed a high premium on schooling but they preferred home-schooling and the children were all educated in this manner. At 18 Thomas started his apprenticeship under his father as an assistant inspector of roads, working mainly on Mitchell's Pass and Bain's Kloof. This period of practical tuition under such an accomplished and inspired engineer gave Thomas a sound foundation on which to build his own illustrious career. The livelihood of father and son continued to be intertwined until Andrew's death in 1864.

By 1854 Thomas was already Inspector of Roads for the Western Province. In that year he married Johanna De Smidt and they enjoyed a long and happy marriage in which they raised 13 children to adulthood. Their first home was the cottage near the summit of what was then called Grey's Pass and is now called Piquenier's Kloof which Thomas was building at the time.

As was the case with his father, Thomas was able to use convict labour in the construction of roads. Thus, in addition to his knowledge of road engineering, he had to be thoroughly conversant with the practical workings of the convict system. To this end he accepted the office of superintendent of convicts. It what might appear as a conflict of interests, he also held the appointment on several occasions of Visiting Magistrate of the convict gangs employed under his general supervision on road works. However it was noted that during the construction of Bain's Kloof the convicts had access to a resident school master, a minister of religion and then weekly visit of a doctor who rode up from Wellington.

His career took a new turn in 1873 with his move to the Railway Department as District Engineer for Wellington but after 18 months, he was recalled to the Roads Department since the authorities could find no suitable replacement to him as a road builder. In 1877, he became an Associate of the Institution of Civil Engineers.

What a busy time he had in the next 20 years! First was Gray's Pass (formerly called Piqueniers 'Piekeniers' Kloof), which opened up the Oliphants River Valley to the Swartland and the Cape Town market, then Tulbagh Kloof and Prince Alfred's Pass (Knysna). This latter followed a 70-kilometre track which crossed the Outeniqua Mountains to connect the Langkloof to Knysna. As the Chief Roads Inspector, a Mr Robinson wrote in a report on Prince Alfred's Pass: "Cutting and felling through a mass of enormous trees, many with trunks of up to 70 feet long and from 25 to 30 feet in girth, clearing these huge trunks and logs away, rooting out the corresponding large stumps and in many places having to blast the road through a most tenacious rock, render it a very tedious and unsatisfactory process."

It was while building Prince Alfred's Pass that Thomas learnt of his father's terminally illness in Cape Town. Apparently he was unable to get leave to visit his dying father, a damning indictment on his superiors. His only diversion was beings asked to take Prince Alfred, Queen Victoria's second son, on an elephant hunt. The 16-year-old prince was then a midshipman on HMS *Euryalus* which in July 1860 paid an official visit to the Cape. Bain accompanied the prince on a hunt at Hartebeeste-Hoek, a farm in the Eastern Cape, resulting in the slaughter of large numbers of game animals. This coincided with the opening of the pass which was duly named after the Prince.

This was followed by the pass from Long Kloof (Avontuur) to Uniondale over the Gwarna Range; Robinson's Pass and the 90-kilometre road from George to Knysna which traversed several mountain passes and many rivers and took 15 years from to complete. Then came the 112-km Tsitsikama road over a series of mountains and rivers which opened up hitherto unchartered Crown land and forests to the public.

With barely a pause for breath, the indomitable Bain tackled the Tradouw Pass; Garcia's Pass; Cogman's Kloof Pass; Molteno Pass and its northern extension towards Carnarvon; De Jager's Pass; Oudekloof Pass; the Great Zwarte Berg Pass (Great Swartberg Pass) which is consider to be Bain's masterpiece. He completed it in three years between 1883 and 1886 with 240 convicts whose only tools were pick axes, crowbars, wheelbarrows, and wagons drawn by draft animals. Although black gun powder was available, preparation for blasting by rock drilling had to be done by hand. Many of the boulders were split by heating them with fire and dousing them with cold water. Rocks were broken into smaller pieces with chisels and sledgehammers and then dressed by convicts working in a chain gang.

Then followed Schoeman's Poort Pass; Baviaans Kloof Road; the deviation in Montagu

Pass making a short cut to George; the reconstruction of Meiring's Poort which was entirely washed away in 1885, the Klein Zwart Berg Road; the Verlaten Kloof and road over the Koodoo Bergen; the Koo mountain pass; the Pakhuis Mountain Pass with its adjuncts towards Calvinia; the Van Rhyn's Pass and its approaches; the high road from Clanwilliam to Namaqualand embracing a series of small mountain passes; Blue Krantz Mountain road; and the Victoria Road from Sea Point to Hout Bay.

These monumental tasks, together with a number of other mountain passes of minor importance and various sections of hard road in the Western and Midland provinces, amounted in aggregate to over 900km, all executed by unskilled convict labour.

The last years of Bain's life were said to have been blighted by a clash of personalities which compelled him to resign. He was then appointed to the post of Irrigation and Geological Surveyor of the Colony in which capacity he designed and completed the Verkeerde Vlei reservoir (affording the Railway Department considerable savings in a providing water service to the Touws River Station); a weir across the Vaal River and a 15km furrow for an irrigation scheme and water supply for the village of Douglas. His talents were also extended to several surveys for large irrigation schemes along the Orange River, for the railway extensions from Port Elizabeth to various centres in the Eastern Cape.

Following his father's interests in geology, he made extensive collections of reptilian remains from the sediment beds of the Karoo for the British and Cape museums, and reported on the mineral resources the Knysna, Prince Albert, Barkly West and Namaqualand goldfields and the coalfields of the Eastern Province and the Free State.

All in all, he completed 45 years' of service, during which he only took one month's leave and the occasional day or two off. Road engineers are traditionally faced with heavy demands on their capacities and Bain soldiered on with his task of completing high-standard road works. However, he paid the price and towards the end he was worn down and in ill-health. Four months after an arduous trip in a small oxcart to investigate suitable irrigation sites near Upington he was dead.

Prince Alfred Pass

12

James Chapman

(1831–1872)

J ames Chapman was a South African explorer, hunter, trader and photographer who, in 1852, ventured across the Limpopo River and into Bamangwato country. He became friendly with Khama, one of the sons of Chief Sekgoma, enlisting his aid in reaching the Chobe River. By 1854 he had teamed up with Samuel H. Edwards, another explorer, and launched an expedition to Lake Ngami. An easy-going man, he was able to get on with the Bushman hunters of the semi-desert interior and spent long periods in their company, obtaining valuable help from them. He explored the Zambezi River to within 70 miles (110 km) of the Victoria Falls, almost beating David Livingstone to his discovery. Returning to Ngami, he travelled north to the Okavango River, crossed Damaraland and reached Walvis Bay.

He wrote *Travels in the interior of South Africa*, (1849-1863): *Hunting and trading journeys from Natal to Walvis Bay* and *Visits to Lake Ngami and Victoria Falls*. Chapman kept diaries throughout his journeys but his book appeared only in 1868, shortly before his death. Edward Tabler, who edited the book from the original manuscript, wrote:

Few South African books give better descriptions of the sport of the country and the habits and customs of the native races inhabiting the vast area traversed, and throughout the volumes there are copious notes on the flora and fauna of the countries visited, amplified by the contents of a valuable index enriched with extracts from the works of able writers.

A son of James Chapman, bookkeeper, teacher and amateur botanist, and Elizabeth Greeff of Malmesbury , his background was a far cry from then aristocratic and well-heeled adventurers of previous pages. He was educated mainly at home and at the age of about 13 left Cape Town to work for a merchant in Durban. Later he opened a trading store at Potchefstroom, where he met Thomas Baines who no doubt inspired him to expand his horizons. He went on hunting trips in the western Transvaal and became an elephant hunter and collected zoological specimens.

No extravagantly equipped expeditions for our James. His treks were financed by the limited proceeds of his trading as a storekeeper. Notwithstanding, his contribution was, as described by Tabler, were significant. In 1852, he crossed the Limpopo River and into Bamangwato country. His friendship with Khama enabled him to reach the Chobe River. Early the following year found him on the Zambesi River which he explored to within 70 miles (110 km) of the Victoria Falls, almost beating David Livingstone to this destination.

According to the S2A3 Biographical Database of Southern African Science:

In 1853 he set off for Matabeleland, accompanied by the missionary Robert Moffat. However, they parted at Shoshong. Chapman went on to hunt in the Lake Ngami region, before returning to Shoshong in October 1854. On his way there he explored unknown territory north-east of the Makarikari Pans and discovered the Gwai River. With the hunter Samuel H. Edwards he set out in November 1854, travelled to the Botletle River and then northwards, reaching the Chinamba Hills (now in the Chobe National Park, Botswana) in January 1855. After hunting there they followed the Botletle River to Lake Ngami (May 1855) where they met Frederick J Green* and JA Wahlberg*, with whom they travelled some distance up the Taokhe River. They then proceeded overland via Ghanzi to Walvis Bay, where they arrived in November 1855. They were the first Europeans to take ox waggons over that route.

During his time with Edwards in the semi-desert interior around Lake Ngami in 1854 he spent long periods in the company of the Bushman hunters who helped him in his hunting exploits.

His next expedition, lasting four years, was with his brother Henry and Thomas Baines. Their goal was to investigate the navigability of the Zambesi River from the Victoria Falls down to its delta. This expedition inspired Baines's paintings of his famous scenes. However, sickness and misfortune put an end to their travels and Chapman returned to Cape Town in 1864, his finances exhausted. Nevertheless, he achieved some recognition through the first ever photographic record of the expedition taken on a stereoscopic camera. Prints of these photographs, unfortunately of poor quality, are on display at the Africana Museum in Johannesburg.

On 12 May 1857 he married Catherine C. Roome, with whom he had two sons and two daughters. In1860 he travelled from Walvis Bay to Lake Ngami, intending to open the

Zambesi River for trade via Hereroland and Lake Ngami. The attempt failed and he wrote a letter to the Governor of the Cape Colony, Sir George Grey, describing his attempt to reach the Zambesi and remarking on the desiccation of the Lake Ngami region. The letter was published as 'Notes on South Africa' in the *Proceedings of the Royal Geographical Society* (1860-1861, Vol. 5, pp. 16-20).

Chapman and Thomas Baines travelled to the upper Zambesi, reaching the Victoria Falls in August 1862 after experiencing many delays and problems. Their journey down the Zambesi River to the East Coast in boats was aborted by malaria, dwindling supplies and heavy rains. He returned to Cape Town in September 1864, in poor health, and for some time worked in the customs department in Cape Town. Subsequently he was appointed superintendent of a convict station for road building in the Knysna district, and then in the George district. He returned to Cape Town in 1868. His *Description of a new species of Quagga from South Africa* was published in the Proceedings of the *Zoological Society of London* in 1865. In 1870 he visited Damaraland and hunted in Ovamboland as far north as the Kunene and Okavango Rivers. The next year he went to the diamond diggings at Du Toit's Pan (now Beaconsfield), near Kimberley, where he died of fever and dysentery in February 1872.

Chapman's fame as one of the greatest explorers of southern Africa rests mainly on his book, a two volume work published in London in 1868. The manuscript was edited, considerably shortened, and republished in 1971.

To quote the *S2A3 Biographical Database of Southern African Science* again:

He was one of the greatest pioneers of his time, and penetrated some areas that had not been visited by Europeans before. He had wide interests (he spoke Tswana and completed vocabularies of several indigenous languages), and good powers of observation. Even though he had no scientific training, the book contains much information about the climate, flora, fauna, and ethnology of the regions visited. As an enthusiastic and knowledgeable naturalist Chapman collected geological specimens, insects, plants, and ethnological material. In 1863 he donated *Coleoptera*, as well as native ornaments and weapons, to the South African Museum, but unfortunately most of the zoological specimens were spoiled. Further presentations were made the next year. He also made a large collection of plants in the neighbourhood of Lake Ngami, but this too suffered much in its long journey to Cape Town.

As mentioned, Chapman was one of the first explorers to use a camera on his travels, from 1860 onwards, and was the first to photograph the desert plant Welwitschia mirabilis.

In November 1867 he was elected a Fellow of the *Royal Geographical Society*. He is commemorated in the name of the plant species *Pancratium chapmanii* and two species of southern African non-marine molluscs, *Stenogyra chapmani* and *Sculptaria chapmanni*, were also named after him.

13

Frederick York St Leger

(1789–1834)

T he original **St Leger** came out from Normandy in 1066 with William the Conqueror. For 500 years the St Legers were sheriffs and Members of Parliament for the County of Kent. Ralph St Leger accompanied Richard 1 on the Third Crusade. Sir Anthony St Leger was granted Leeds Castle by Edward VI in 1550. His second son, Warham was knighted and became Governor of Munster. His grandson, who was a friend of Sir Walter Raleigh, was mentioned in Kingsley's "Westward Ho" and is one of the boys in John Millais' painting, *The Boyhood of Raleigh*.

An especially distinguished member of the family was Sir Thomas St Leger, Sheriff of Surrey and Ambassador to France. He married Anne, sister of Edward 1V, but paid the penalty of the royal connection when he was executed in 1483 after Richard 111 came to the throne. The St Leger Stakes were founded in 1776, four years before the Derby, by Major-General Anthony St Leger and his portrait by Gainsborough is hanging in Buckingham Palace.

The founder of the South African branch, Frederick York St Leger, is my great grandfather on my mother's side.

He was born in Limerick in 1833. To quote Moya Frenz St Leger (*St Leger: The Family and the Race*): *The Irish troubles of the 1840s led to the family's removal from Ireland to Monmouthshire, a move which is believed to have caused Frederick's mother, Jane, such chronic homesickness that she slowly wasted away. In 1843, she took her three youngest children on a visit to her father's home in Ballyally, Co Clare, where she died 'of a broken heart'.*

Frederick had very little to do with his father, which is just as well as the family legend has it, he fell on bad times through standing surety for a near relative. This reduced him to working as a clerk in the P & O shipping line for the rest of his active life. Frederick, now a motherless but highly intelligent 10-year old, was sent to live with his learned uncle, the Rev William Nassau St Leger, Vicar of *St Mary-le-Tower* in Ipswich. He was swathed in an atmosphere of learning which led to an enduring love of the classics. A scholarship provided him with the entree to *Corpus Christi College*, Cambridge where he distinguished himself as the gold medallist in the *Classical Tripos*. Tripos (listen) distinguishes the different kinds of bachelor's degrees at Cambridge. An undergraduate studying the classics is thus said to be reading for the *Classical Tripos,* whilst a student of English is reading for the *English Tripos*. The word has an obscure etymology, but may be traced to the three-legged stool candidates once used to sit on when taking oral examinations. An apocryphal legend says that students used to receive one leg of a stool in each of their three years of exams, receiving the whole stool at the completion of their studies.

After graduating, he took up a post as classics master at Oundle School, located in the ancient market town of Oundle in Northamptonshire. The school was founded by Sir William Laxton, a member of the Worshipful Company of Grocers who became Lord Mayor of London in 1544, during the reign of Henry VIII. Laxton used the prosperity which his life in London had granted him to establish a school for the local boys of Oundle. There had been a school on the site since at least as early as 1485, and is still regarded as one of the finest co-educational British public schools. The head master was Mungo Park, a great-nephew of the famous African explorer who was credited as being the first Westerner to encounter the Niger River.

It was at Oundle that Frederick York St Leger met and married Christian Emma Muddle whose father was a purser in the East India Company. Shortly after, FY and his young wife were fired with the dream of starting a new life in the colonies. He must have harboured some religious zeal in his bosom as he sailed to the Cape in 1856 at the age of 24 with his young wife, responding to the urgent call from Bishop Gray for missionaries to strengthen the Anglican Church. Gray was the son of Robert Gray, Bishop of Bristol, who ordained him deacon in Wells Cathedral in 1834. As a priest he was interested in mission, and was local secretary for the Society for the Propagation of the Gospel in Foreign Parts. In 1847, he was ordained Bishop of Cape Town in Westminster Abbey, the first bishop of the Anglican Church in South Africa. He arrived in his *Oundle School* diocese, the boundaries of which were undefined, the following year. Soon after, he set out on a journey to explore his diocese, accompanied by James Green, who was to be rector of Pietermaritzburg in the Colony of Natal.

At that time there were only 13 Anglican congregations, no church schools and no missions. He was determined that this should change, especially as the Methodist Church was in a far healthier position. The missionary of the Society for the Propagation of the Gospel, Bishop Armstrong, on the eve of his departure to the Cape in July 1854, delivered a speech which indicates the current beliefs of the Anglican community in those days:

I go forth in a few days with the very first missionaries of the Church of England for that Kafir race with whom we have been in intercourse for the last fifty years. If the Kafirs abound in the diocese of Grahamstown by thousands, the Church of England has yet done nothing for them. She has not yet spent one farthing: she has not sent one missionary; she has not formed one mission-station. Look at the religious state of these Kafirs. It is not an ordinary state. We cannot go among them as the apostle of the Gentiles in olden days, and point to the altar to the Unknown God, and beginning with natural religion, already confessed among them, unfold to them from that the blessed mysteries of Christ. They are without a God, true or false. They have no worship whatever. They have no word in their language which represents any idea, however imperfect or however mistaken, of any Supreme Being that has love and goodness as His attributes. And therefore is there not given to us the glorious privilege of teaching them that there is not only a God in heaven, but One too Who, in the fullness of His unspeakable love, has sent forth His only- begotten Son, that dark souls may look up to Him for light, and life, and immortality, and resurrection, from the dead? This is the condition of the Kafirs, and it is from this fearful, unnatural, and godless condition, that it is our privilege to raise them, if we will only do our work in time.

FY took up residence in Grahamstown and in a letter to the Reverend E Hawkins, at the end of which he signed himself John Grahamstown; he recorded:

... the laying of the foundation-stone of our infant college, which I dedicated to St. Andrew, as on St. Andrew's Day. I received consecration. It was altogether a bright day in our annals. The clergy in their surplices, with Archdeacon Merriman at their head, moved in procession, with a large body of lay people, to the site of the chapel, where the Lieutenant-Governor and his staff were waiting. There, joining the clergy, I accompanied them to the place prepared. The service was a very solemn one; a large concourse of people appeared to take a lively interest in the undertaking; and when the stone was laid, we all proceeded in due order to the cathedral for evening prayer, which a large congregation attended. The college is now rapidly rising, and, if all is well, will be open in a few months.

At the time he was appointed headmaster, the school was In its infancy with only 12 small boys. According to the college records the numbers started to rise almost immediately, as a result of his confidence in deciding to build classrooms and a dormitory. By the time he left, three years later, the school register had swelled to over 50 pupils. His granddaughter, Jean St Leger Lawrence recorded years later:

I was not able to establish the stipend for the principal in those initial years, but one of the two masters under him received '£50 per annum less board and lodging of £30 per annum!' St Leger was a fine young headmaster and left an indelible mark upon the school and, indeed, his family was destined to continue the link with Grahamstown through the years. His two youngest children, Ellen and Anthony, married and lived there; of his many highly gifted grandsons and great-grandsons, quite a number have won their first distinctions at St Andrew's College; and a great-grand -daughter is married to Canon Aubrey, the headmaster.

RF Currey, who was headmaster of St Andrew's from 1939 to 1955, writes of St Leger in his *History of St Andrew's College* as follows:

With St Leger one realises that those influences on a man which 'gentle his condition' are being brought to bear, at the first moment that circumstances made such influence possible, on St Andrew's boys. He was himself a Classic of the first order. Indeed, a polished translation of the Second Eclogue on a slip of paper, yellow with age, tucked into the pages of his mark book, may claim to be the first addition to English poetry that has come from St Andrew's. It is clear that St Leger, too, had to struggle against financial difficulties of the gravest kind.

Bishop Cotterill, addressing the first Diocesan Synod in 1861, referred to St Andrew's *in which boys may now receive an education such as in England can only be obtained in the best grammar schools.*

Visitors to St Andrew's College today can view a stone pergola which was a gift from Anthony York St Leger. The inscription reads:

This pergola commemorates the services to St Andrew's and South Africa of Frederick York St Leger MA Cantab (1833-1901) second headmaster of this College and of his grandson, Frederick Anthony St Leger of this school and Rhodes University College who died, aged 32 years, on 12 September 1942 at Benghazi as POW serving in SA Artillery.

One gave long years with heart and brain
One youth's brief glorious blows
For freedom: whence the greater gain
Only the Master knows.

FY, after tenure of five years in Grahamstown, was appointed Rector of St Michael's and Headmaster of St Michael's School in Queenstown. This followed the shifting of the frontier between the two opposing communities to the Kei River. Canon Matthew Morton described him as one of the cleverest men in the diocese "but not an orator".

In 1867, only 34 years of age, he was appointed canon and accompanied Bishop Cotterill, Bishop of Grahamstown, as his chaplain on a visit to England. On his departure, St Leger was presented with a purse of 150 guineas by his congregation. He brought back with him the following year a fine set of stained glass windows which can today be viewed in the apse of the new St Michael's in Queenstown. In 1870 Frederick York represented the Grahamstown diocese at the first provincial synod of the Church of the Province of South Africa. At this historic gathering at which the constitution of the Church was drawn up, FY was appointed Secretary of the Synod. Many thought the young man was a potential candidate for the bishopric himself.

In 1871, at the age of 38, in an extraordinary change of course, he resigned his living with the church and took his family to the newly-opened diamond fields in Kimberley. To quote Moya St Leger again:

> Man is not solely a rational being and FY's action is consistent with many odd decisions taken by St Legers who have broken away from the routine and ritual of the settled life, like birds escaping from a cage.

There is no written record of his resignation in the archives at Bishopscourt but it is assumed that he found it impossible to provide for his family on the small stipend that the church paid. The St Legers had seven children - Fred (14), John (12), Jane (8), Robert (6), Stratford (3) and Ellen Mary (1). A seventh child, Anthony York, was to be born in Kimberley two years later.

His decision to leave might also have been due to his wife converting to the Roman Catholic faith. However, this did not affect his own religious convictions and he remained a committed Anglican until his death. Another possible reason for FY's leaving the church was the Bishop Colenso crisis. The Right Reverend Dr John William Colenso was the first bishop of the English Church in Natal and was distinguished almost from his arrival by "a very warm attachment to the Bantu, combined with an untiring zeal for their improvement and an eloquent advocacy for what he regarded as their rights." Jean St Leger Lawrence recorded:

> The controversy of the 1860s which ended in the trial of Colenso on a charge of heresy and led to the split in the Anglican Church in South Africa, affected my grandfather profoundly, and he kept copies of his long, and abstruse (sic) correspondence with Bishop Gray up on this issue. When my mother, his eldest daughter, died, we children made little of the fine, faded hand-writing upon endless sheets of yellowing notepaper. We consigned grandfather's letters to a bonfire, and that was that. We passed on to the mountain of family photographs and burnt them, too. And after that my father s diaries. Youth must press forward, there is no time to go back, we told each other. And I expect we were right.

Colenso incensed his more orthodox peers by publishing a work of biblical criticism. Called upon to retract his opinions, he declined to do so and was summoned to appear before a court composed of all the South African bishops. Colenso, whose bishopric over the See of Natal was created by letters patent signed by the Queen, refused to accept the authority of the court of South African Bishops. They pronounced him guilty of heresy and sentenced him to be deposed. He ignored their judgement and appealed to the highest tribunal in England which upheld his position. The colonial churches were declared to be nothing more than voluntary associations bound by no law to the established Church of England. The Bishops promptly consecrated Dr WK Macrorie who took the title of Bishop of Maritzburg of the Church of the Province of South Africa. Bishop Colenso continued in his position to the delight of the natives in his congregation and to the understandable chagrin of his peers in Cape Town. This whole episode did not sit lightly with St Leger's classical Christian faith. However, this must be the subject of another story. Our narrative moves on to the Diamond Fields.

Diamonds, of course, are the stuff of legends. As we have already read, the first diamond was found in the Orange River in the Hopetown district. The story goes that a farmer, Schalk van Niekerk, happened to call on a neighbour by the name of Jacobs and observed the children playing with a remarkably brilliant pebble. Mrs Jacobs presented him with the stone. A short while later, van Niekerk showed his trophy to a trader called O'Reilly who immediately suspected it was a diamond. He took it to the Clerk of the Peace, Lorenzo Boyes who was well aware of the keen interest in geology of Dr Guybon Atherstone (the subject of a previous chapter). So it was, then, that in March 1867 Dr Atherstone received through the Post Office a letter containing the Hopetown 'pebble'.

The discovery of diamonds brought a wave of prospectors to the Northern Cape. The whole of the colonies and the independent states were in such a wretchedly depressed condition, according to the historian George McCall Theal that a large proportion of the population was ready to embark on any enterprise that would provide subsistence. In the years that followed, mechanics and clerks, professional men and labourers, farmers and merchants, all imagined that fortunes were to be made on the banks of the Vaal.

And so, to quote Jean Lawrence again, we find FY:

… taking passage for Kimberley with his long-suffering wife and seven children; in Cobb's Coach, stopping overnight in bitter cold at Burghersdorp, Bethulie and Fauresmith. My uncle Bob who was six years old at the time, recalled to the end of his days the teeming game on either side of their road and the sight of farmers riding across the veld in pursuit or herds of springbok, which they shot from the saddle. The family moved into quarters in Main Street, New Rush Camp - one small wooden hut and a large tent. They slept in hammocks. The kitchen was a hole in the ground, in the centre of which stood a three-legged black pot in which all meals were cooked. Water, at 8/6 a bucket, had to be fetched from the wells. Kimberley, being at that time, of course, a town of pioneers, there was not a single brick building; if a dwelling was sold, a gang of natives would pick it up and carry it to its new site - it was a common occurrence for the excited little St. Legers to see a house walking down the street. Little help being available in the event of sickness, my grandmother very wisely kept a medicine chest well-stocked with pills, etc. for every emergency. One day a runaway cart and horse charged down the Main Street and through the St Leger home, parting the hut from the tent and scattering the contents of the medicine chest upon the ground. By the time the alarm was over small grubby hands had scooped up every sugar-coated pills and the little tummies were distended with remedies. I believe there were no results, either good or bad!

As if this new, rough life were not enough to contend with, Mrs St Leger gave birth before the year was out to her eighth child, Anthony - a delicate boy who had to be fed upon asses milk. His brothers never let him forget this, but he outlived them all! The ex-clergyman supported his family quite easily on his writings; for which he showed a remarkable talent in one who had never been trained to journalism, but the new baby did not thrive in the mining town.

Ivan Mitford-Barberton recorded the situation thus:

Chaos and squalour characterised the settlements at the New Rush camp at Kimberley. Thirty thousand men, white and black, swarmed over the claims in the Kimberley, Dorstfontein and Bultfontein mines. Within a short while a great galvanised iron town sprang up, with a canteen at every corner. The main mine was a vast hole into which thousands of wire ropes were stretched from windlasses mounted in tiers on the surface. Running on these wires were thousands of iron and leather buckets, hauling up loads of blue gravel. At the bottom of the mine were thousands of busy workers toiling like ants amid a cacophony of sounds – the thud of their picks, the groan and creaking of their windlasses, the rattle of iron wheels upon steel ropes and the songs and shouts.

The bad water, the filth, the dust storms and the vermin brought on discomfort and sickness. It may have been a blessing that Frederick's constitution was unable to cope with these conditions and after a spell as a diamond buyer he turned to writing articles for the newspapers and was able to move his family to more civilised habitation.

In 1873 he was offered the editorship of *The Diamond Fields*. For the next two years, Frederick York was one of the most knowledgeable and accomplished journalists in Kimberley and his articles were published in newspapers across the country and overseas. However, he was always sensitive when it came to his professional integrity, and he resigned after a dispute with the proprietors in 1875.

Now was the time to enjoy the fruits of a more civilised life and he accepted an invitation from the proprietors of the newly-formed *Daily News* in Cape Town to edit their newspaper. They set out for Cape Town, travelling partly by Gibson's Coach but mainly by ox-wagon to the railhead at Wellington, spending the nights at Hopetown, Britstown and Beaufort West en route. It was the spring of 1875; after the dry Karoo they were enchanted with the streets of Beaufort West, bordered with fruit tree in blossom and with streams of clear water trickling beneath.

Soon, however, Frederick York was again faced with what he believed to be improper interference by the owners and he resigned rather than write an article on instructions. In an ambitious - some might say foolhardy - venture, he founded his own newspaper, The *Cape Times*. The first edition, a modest four- pager of small format, was published on 27

March 1876. Strong in idealism and scholarship but singularly lacking in capital and financial acumen, Frederick York was surely embarking on a risky venture.

Jean Lawrence:

For day beforehand, the big event had been heralded with variegated posters stuck up over the town; and in honour of the occasion each vendor was given a new straw hat to wear, with *Cape Times* printed on the ribbon. The *Cape Times* never looked back. My maternal grandfather's leading articles were forceful, to say the least, and the journal caught the imagination of the citizens of Cape Town from the start. His paper prospered and soon the young editor and his family moved out to make their home at Rosebank.

It was a hand-to-mouth existence and for many years the enterprise was chronically under-capitalised. But St Leger was no slouch as a worker. He would normally spend the mornings in his office in St George's Street, reading and writing letters and preparing articles for publication. After lunch, he would take his place in the Press Gallery of Parliament promptly at 2.30 and would spend the afternoon there listening to the debates and writing his Notes in the House (a feature continued by subsequent editors and columnists of the likes of Victor Norton, Angus McKenzie, Anthony Delius and John Scott). What distinguished FY from his successors, of course, was that he dashed off his notes ready for the printer while the debate continued. On a quiet afternoon, he would write reviews of books he had previously read at home. After an early dinner with his wife and children, he would return to Parliament by 8pm if there was a night sitting, or he would write his editorials in his office until it was time to read the proofs that were sent round from Thomas Delahunt's printing works where every letter of type was set by hand and illustrations were confined to line engravings.

The popularity of the newspaper grew rapidly. It was the first in the country to make use of the telegraph to gather news, until then carried by mail steamer or post cart. The policy to which FY adhered faithfully throughout his career was based on his conviction that 'liberty indeed is so far a law of nature to us, individually and nationally, that once the state of dependence is passed, there can be no moral or political health without it.' From the outset he aimed at making the newspaper an honest record of public opinion, 'not the journal of a particular party, but of colonists as a whole.'

Gerald Shaw, in his book (*Early Beginnings: Cape Times 1876-1910*), described the man who was to be editor for the next 20 years as:

aloof and reserved, with little taste for general society. As a rule, he shunned close contact with politicians. However, he enjoyed club life and was a founder member of the City Club. Over the years, he was to become a well-known figure, immaculate in spats and topper and sporting a silver-headed cane. He wore Victorian side-whiskers and carried himself with military bearing. He was ever gentle in speech and his grey-blue eyes were often sparked with humour. His knowledge of the Bible and the classics were so strong after more than three decades that he was still able to quote whole passages, which he frequently did in his editorial columns, entirely from memory.

CAL Green, a reporter who worked for the Cape Times, recalls that the Old Saint (as he came to be known to his staff) was a most polished writer. He had a retentive memory and an unusually high regard for accuracy. While he appeared aloof, it was due to shyness rather than to any intellectual arrogance. James Rose-Innes, a close friend who was to become Attorney General, said that FY's *opinions, his scholarship and delicate fancy impersonally permeated his paper.* He wrote for cultivated men and although his style might appear ornate by contemporary standards, it reflected his oblique and ironic personality. Victor Samson, a freelance reporter, recalled that *it was the wit and brilliant writing of St Leger that made the leaders in the paper a joy in the mornings to anyone who appreciated the Saint's good things.*

His family continued to enjoy the comfort and security of their beautiful home. They attended the best schools, mixed with the other children of the best families and generally made the best of marriages, with the church, the professions and the regiments figuring prominently. A little-known chapter of his life was his service as a major in Duke of Edinburgh's Own Volunteer Rifles, the first volunteer unit in the Cape, founded in 1855 as the Cape Rifle Corps. In 1867 Prince Alfred, Duke of Edinburgh accorded it the title 'Duke of Edinburgh's Own', after it had formed a guard of honour for him during a visit to Cape Town. According to Jean St Leger Lawrence, St Leger served with the regiment in the Basuto War in 1880 although no details have been recorded. (Basutoland was under the nominal control of the Cape but the chiefs rebelled in 1880 when part of their territory was surveyed for white settlement and at the same time they were called upon to surrender their firearms). Colonial Cape forces sent to put down the rebellion suffered heavy casualties, as the Basotho had obtained serviceable firearms from the Orange Free State and enjoyed a natural defensive advantage in their country's mountainous terrain. The rebels relied primarily on guerrilla warfare, ambushing isolated units to negate the British/ Cape superiority in firepower. In October, Basotho forces ambushed a mounted column of British Army lancers at Qalabani - present-day Lancers Gap near Maseru - killing 39. The defeat of an experienced and well-armed cavalry column discouraged Cape authorities.

The *Cape Times* grew steadily in stature and influence to become the leading newspaper in South Africa by the early 1890s. FY's editorial policy was at times fiercely independent. He scorned the rival *Cape Argus* when it came out in mourning with black borders after the defeat of the British at Isandhlwana. He described the Boer victory at Majuba 'a salutary lesson in political wisdom for the Gladstone Ministry instilled into them by the sharp-shooting of a few rock-protected marksmen'.

He accepted with equanimity, if not with enthusiasm, the recognition of Dutch as a language in Parliament while noting that English was not accorded similar privileges in the Orange Free State. When Cecil Rhodes became Prime Minister of the Cape Colony in 1890, with the support of the Afrikaner Bond, St Leger questioned the wisdom of the appointment of a man who wielded such immense power outside the House. Rhodes was Chairman of De Beers, Consolidated Goldfields and the British South Africa Company.

While praising his remarkable achievements and his *noble ambition, far above a mere passion for gain,* St Leger nevertheless foresaw a potential conflict of interests.

Two quotations from Mark Twain from his book *Diamonds* are relevant here:

> Next to Mr Rhodes, to me the most interesting convulsion of nature in South Africa was the diamond crater – and; Towering above us was Table Mountain: a reminder that we had now seen each and all of the great features of South Africa except Mr Cecil Rhodes. I realise that that is a large exception—he is the only un-royal outsider whose arrival in London can compete with an eclipse.

FY's views were generally not shared by his fellow editors and in the 1890s he brought an action against the publishers of the *Kaffrarian Watchman* in King William's Town which accused the *Cape Times* (our bilious contemporary) of manipulating reports of Parliamentary proceedings, of *supressio veri* and *suggestio falsi.* James Rose Innes appeared for St Leger together with MW (later Sir Malcolm) Searle who was to marry FY's daughter, Emma Jane. The judgement, as was to be expected, went in his favour but he refused to press for damages, and simply desired to clear his name.

This was the subject of a humorous article in Cape Punch on 22 February 22, 1888 entitled *St Cape Times.*

> It was a busy scene. Printers' devils flew hither and thither with copy, with proofs, and with revises. The steam engine was hissing and snorting, burning to be at work; the great machine lay in the shade ready to receive the "formes," there was a hammering of furniture as the outsides were being locked up, a rushing of feet, and din and turmoil reigned supreme. And why? A great morning daily was prepared for light. In a few hours its hundreds of thousands of readers would be gazing upon its pages laden deep with wisdom, with prescience, and with wit.
>
> But the motive power of this great commotion sat in his office, a few doors higher up the street, his brow wrinkled with care, his eyes brimful of unshed tears, while a convulsive sob would break forth from his agitated frame. In one hand he held a handkerchief, whilst in the other, which rested upon the table, he held a photograph upon which he was gazing.
>
> "Oh, Blewett, faithless, unfeeling Blewett," he murmured, "who would have thought that you could have done such a thing?" "Ah, Mr. Cape-Punch, " he added, as the Illustrious One entered, "was it not cruel?"
>
> "Cruel, Mr. St Cape Times," responded Mr. O.-P., "to what may you refer?"
>
> "To what may I refer, repeated the unhappy gentleman slowly and incredulously, "to what may I refer?" Is it possible that you have not heard of it?" And he broke into fresh sobs.
>
> "Heard of what?" enquired his friend. "Calm yourself a moment and explain."
>
> "Of the articles in the Kaffrarian Bobby. Those cruel, unkind, bitter, biting, insinuating articles?"

"I must own to the soft impeachment. I confess that I have not yet seen or heard of these articles."

"No-well, then listen," and slowly unfolding a copy of the Kaffrarian Bobby, which was damp with tears, he read in a broken voice : "The complaint assumed a very virulent form, and remains so up to the present, black spots of 'moral obliquity', presenting themselves without intermission to the editorial sight. And to this we owe the wholly unreliable character of the Cape Time's parliamentary reports and assertions in its leading columns."

When he had finished reading these extracts he lay back in his chair and gazed at a picture on the wall opposite and his manner was such that Mr C-P came to the conclusions that he was drawing long draughts of consolation from the sight. This is what is referred to as "editorial sight".

"Really," replied Mr Cape-Punch, " may I look at it?"

Mr St Cape Times nodded assent, and the Great Colonist turned in his chair and gazed upon a PACHYDERM. There was no mistaking It. It was the exact representation of a Pachyderm. When Mr O.-P. resumed his former position, there was a wondering sort of look upon his face which his companion immediately noticed.

"That Pachyderm is symbolical of our calling," the Editor explained, "and although I have never known what it was before this to have unkind things said of me, yet I have always kept that hanging there to remind me of the thick skins of statesmen and others, so that I may be encouraged to level my bolts at them. And now! To think that I should have lived to see the day when my fondest belief should be shattered into a thousand fragments. I always thought that journalists never said hard things of each other, that they, at least, were free from the small spite which distinguishes other callings, that envy never filled their breasts, and misrepresentation had no place therein. And now –oh Blewett, Blewett, how could you?" And a fresh burst of weeping relieved the poor gentleman's overwrought feelings.

"But, my dear Sir," exclaimed Mr Cape-Punch, deeply touched at his friend's grief, "No one for a moment believed these reports. If you will allow Mr Cape Punch to express an opinion - an opinion shared by several thousands of his fellow-colonists - it is to this effect: The Parliamentary reports which have appeared in your paper are widely appreciated, are looked forward to with Interest, and are a credit to the press of the Colony, and no one for a moment imagines them to be cooked; while the parliamentary notes are as delightful reading as may be found in any Colonial journal - excepting, of course, in the columns of Cape Punch."

"Of course!" exclaimed the editor, with a grateful look on his face. "Then you really think that that cruel Blewett has not injured me in the estimation of my fellows in the slightest degree?"

"I am confident of it!" replied Mr. O.-P., taking his hat. "Then" exclaimed Mr St Cape Time,"Begone, dull care! I am once more a pachydermatous journalist! "

On his retirement in June, 1895, FY reluctantly accepted the advice of his son Fred, who was business manager of the newspaper, that Dr Rutherfoord Harris, Fred's brother- in-law, should put some capital into the company. FY, as we have seen, distrusted the potential and actual interference of shareholders and was probably not very enamoured of his new partner.

Harris had been a doctor in Kimberley and an early associate of Cecil Rhodes, becoming Secretary of the British South Africa Company. Several years later Harris secured Rhodes' re-election as MP for Barkly West in circumstances which led to a petition for the result to be set aside on the grounds of bribery. The petition was not successful but the Chief Justice, Lord de Villiers, described Harris' conduct as very reprehensible. In the interim, St Leger had insisted on a deed of partnership which stipulated that the newspaper's policy and editorial control should not be affected. He had chosen his successor as editor, a young English journalist, Edward Garrett who was, predictably, severely pressurised by Harris to promote the interests of Rhodes (who had already acquired control of the Cape Argus and the Johannesburg Star.)

FY, on his retirement, became a Town Councillor and joined Rose Innes' SA Political Association whose liberal views (including the abolition of protective duties on foodstuffs) were opposed by Rhodes in deference to his parliamentary ally, the Afrikaner Bond which had a strong farming constituency. The Jameson Raid brought Rhodes down and FY sought election to the Legislative Council (the Upper House). But he developed a painful affliction of the throat and was not successful. The following year he was elected the member for Cape Town in the Legislative Assembly and he took his place in Parliament. However he was hardly able to speak and travelled to England to consult a specialist who diagnosed cancer.

FY presided as Chairman at the first annual general meeting of the Cape Times in its new guise as a limited liability company. The other directors were ER Syfret, representing Harris' 41 per cent interest, and TE Fuller. He also took his seat in the 1899 session of the Cape Parliament but was in great pain and unable to speak in the House. In October the Anglo- Boer War broke out and MP's returned to their constituencies to seek peace.

St Leger was now slowly dying of cancer, but it was tragically prolonged. A tracheotomy was performed a year later which brought some respite but for the next five months as his condition deteriorated, he listened to sacred and classical music played by his wife. He died at his home, Clyst Hazel in Newlands, on 28 March 1901 at the age of 68.

His funeral was attended by many dignitaries, including the Prime Minister, Sir Gordon Sprigg. In his will, he left his shares to his children, only to be inherited after the death of his wife. Edmund Garrett paid the following tribute to his late comrade:

> This is not the place to dwell on his political teachings - a high-minded Imperialism with a strong vein of Christian socialism - but of his public work let me say this: not a newspaper writer among us but is the better for it, the better able to rise above all that is tawdry or servile or unchivalrous. It means much for the broadening river of South

African journalism that it flowed near the source with so pure a stream.

In 1902 there was unveiled a tablet to his memory "over the pew which he occupied for 15 years" in St George's Cathedral. It was donated by the employees of the Cape Times and is inscribed with the family motto of the St Legers: "Haut at Bon".

FY's son Fred withdrew from his position as manager and an agreement was drawn up in terms of which he was to go overseas for 12 months on full pay and "devote some of his attention to the inspection of modern machinery and newspaper working". He was also urged to "take steps to free himself of his private financial liabilities" and "withdraw from all connection with horse racing". Whether he complied with these conditions is not clear but he remained on the Board of Directors until 1935, from time to time expressing his dissatisfaction with the quality of the newspaper's racing coverage.

An obituary on FY published in his newspaper on 3 April 1901, stated that:

...in expressing a sense of personal pain and sorrow at his departure we are but voicing the sentiments of every member of this community, and those of a very wide circle of friends and admirers in all parts of South Africa. ...With the death of Mr St Leger there passes from our midst a spirit·of rare worth and refinement. It was given to but few outside the immediate family circle, to understand and appreciate at their proper value and in their true perspective the characteristics which harmonised in so perfect a degree in the personality of the late senior member for Cape Town. His innate reticence, his disinclination of general society, and his abhorrence of anything which could, even in the smallest degree, savour of self- assertiveness or personal advertisement created for him a position distinct and unique, and by the same token concealed from the general view those delightful phases of his interesting personality which were well known to and so highly prized by those who were privileged to come into daily contact with him, or to share, in however small a degree, his confidence and friendship. To the bulk of the general public Mr. St. Leger appeared as a quiet, unobtrusive, dignified, self-contained man, caring little for general outside friendships, absorbed in the work of his life, seeking not public applause, but public progress and happiness - a man of high culture and refinement, of keen susceptibilities of wide sympathies and deep feeling, content to discharge his daily task like any other labourer in the field of the world's work. Those who knew him best could appreciate him most, and rightly valued his friendship and confidence, could rejoice at the privilege which was theirs. These, we say, were comparatively few, for St. Leger never gave his confidence save after long association and proved reliability. But once given, that confidence was rarely withdrawn. This circle of friends will mourn his departure with sincere sorrow: But they will derive comfort from the reflection that they were so privileged, and in the knowledge that the life's labours of their friend and co-worker can have not but an abiding influence for good upon the future of South. Africa.

As editor of the Cape Times for 25 years, he wielded immense power and great influence in the political councils of the Colony and South Africa as a whole. He fully recognized the responsibilities which this unique position brought him .....and was never swayed by one ignoble consideration. He never had anything to conceal; he was never influenced by ulterior motives; he had a natural horror of sham; his only aim was seeking to advance the highest political, moral and material welfare of the community.

Bishop Robert Gray

John William Colenso

George McCall Theal

FY St Leger in later years

Mark Twain

James Rose Innes

St Andrew's College

The front page of the first edition of the Cape Times

The diamond diggings at Kimberley-Kopje in 1872, drawn by J. Vanione,
Emil Holub's "Seven Years in South Africa" published in Vienna, 1881

"The Boyhood of Raleigh" by John Millais

Oundle School

Cape Town City Club

14

Albert Victor Lindbergh

(1872–1939)

Albert Victor Lindbergh, the founder of the *Central News Agency*, came into the St Leger circle in 1892. AVL as he was generally known, was the grandson of a respected judge in Stockholm and the son of a captain in the merchant marine. However, his mother was Welsh and he grew up there. He was a bright lad and successful at school. He was destined to become a teacher when he was introduced to the editor of the *Cardiff Times* who, impressed with the young man's clarity and vision, asked him to write a series of articles on South Africa, in particular the newly established town of Johannesburg. He was given a letter of introduction to FY. He sailed to the Cape on the *SS Tantallen Castle* together with several hundred emigrants in steerage, mostly miners from Cornwall seeking their fortunes in Kimberley and Johannesburg, and no doubt he shared their dreams of a fortune to be made in their new country. Several days after arriving in Cape Town, AVL sought an interview with the editor and owner of Cape Town's most esteemed newspaper. The office of the *Cape Times* in St George's Street was a three-storey building with a Tudor gable, a colonial coat of arms and the motto *Spes Bona* prominently displayed on the façade.

Madeleine Masson, in her biography of AVL described the meeting thus:

> The two men shaking hands had not the slightest inkling of what fate had in store for them, and that one day the blood in the veins of Frederick York St Leger would flow in the veins of Albert Victor's children and their descendants... AVL was invited to tea at the editor's home, Cyst Hazel, in Claremont where he met other members of the St

Leger family including the eldest son, Frederick Luke, his wife and two of their little daughters, one of whom, a pretty flaxen haired toddler in her white glace kid boots was to become his adored wife Gladdie.

Having met and made a good impression on the editor of *The Star* in Johannesburg, he was placed in charge of the circulation department. He had already formed a close friendship with young Michael Davis who had set up a small enterprise as a street corner newspaper seller. From this partnership, the *Central News Agency* was born – soon to be publishers of the *Natal Mercury, Star, Transvaal Leader, Rand Daily Mail, Sunday Times, Cape Times, Cape Argus, SA News, SA Lady's Pictorial, Bloemfontein Post, Friend, Pretoria News* etc. as well as 'Importers of the World Periodicals, Wholesale Stationers and Booksellers, Railway Bookstore Contractors, Advertisement Contractors for the World Press, Authorised Agents for all Government Publications'.

With the outbreak of the Anglo-Boer war, AVL met the young Rudyard Kipling who's *Just So* stories were said to be written on the Limpopo. Lord Roberts, before assuming command of the army, sent for Kipling to plan a newspaper for the troops. This resulted in the Friend in Bloemfontein being taken over for this purpose with AVL being responsible for distribution.

AVL also met Richard Horatio Edgar Wallace, a foreign correspondent for the *Reuters News Agency*. He subsequently became the first editor of a newspaper when Harry Freeman Cohen, the wealthy stockbroker, bought the moribund *Standard & Digger News*, and launched it under a new title – the *Rand Daily Mail*. However, the editor's flamboyant style and extravagant promotional projects soon resulted in Wallace's job being terminated and it was only through Abe Bailey's financial intervention that this publication survived. Bailey leased the *Rand Daily Mail* to a syndicate of three – AVL, Ralph Ward-Jackson and George Kingswell.

The following history of the *CNA* group is taken from the Bruwer Survey, courtesy of the Heritage Department of the City of Johannesburg: CENTRAL NEWS AGENCY (1886 - 1898) Today, *CNA* is one of the biggest book and stationery retailers in the country. But their start was a humble one, in the newspaper and publishing business a little over 100 years ago. In 1896 two entrepreneurs, Michael Davis and Albert Lindbergh, paired up to sell newspapers on the dusty streets of the Johannesburg. The first newspapers sold were *The Star, The Standard* and *Diggers News*. Davis and Lindbergh soon moved into the sale of books, periodicals and stationery and began acting as advertising agents. Newspapers, however, were their greatest interest.

AVL maintained close contact with FY St Leger and his son Frederick and was a frequent guest at their respective homes. It was no surprise to the families when AVL, although in his 40s, declared his love for Gladys who was 17 years his junior. They were married in 1913; their wedding being a social event which brought together guests from the press, politics and finance as well as members of the leading Cape families.

VERITAS·OMNIA·VINCIT

BARBER

Part Two

The account of some of my
illustrious ancestors and how their lives
made history in their time.

15

Barbers of the Peak

As recorded by **Ivan Mitford-Barberton** (1896-1976) in his book *Barbers of the Peak*, our family dates back to the dim Middle Ages, to the wild and rugged vastness of the Great Peak in Derbyshire. We are of Norman origin, said to have come from the town of Sainte- Barbe sur-Gallon in France and certain members of the clan are recorded on the Battle Abbey Roll with other followers of William the Conqueror. In the deep forests and untamed mountains of the Great Peak, far from the civilizing influences of the industrial centres, lived the great Barber clan, toiling, pioneering and settling the waste places. In the 11th and 12th centuries the name stood high in rank dignity, none more so than Henry Barber, Lord of the Peak.

The Barbers spread out, in the ensuing centuries, to settle in the wilds of Yorkshire, the Lincolnshire fens, the Berkshire granaries, the Leicestershire mills, the Staffordshire potteries and other neighbouring counties. One family moved to London, and at an early date a Barber occupied the lofty position of Lord Mayor. It is from that family that Charles Barber, the Calcutta merchant, is descended. When he died, in

1799, he owned extensive properties, warehouses and shops. He left everything to his mother Margaret Barber who, unbeknown to him, had died a month or two before. Charles' brother George, a useless sort of fellow, was lost in India and never traced. The Government advertised for relatives to come and claim the money - and the clan of Barber rose as one man. Every Barber In the kingdom thought he had a claim and, after a lot of sifting, a certain amount of money was paid out in 1801. But about a quarter of a million pounds was held in Chancery and despite a subsequent legal action against the Government in an attempt to get the money 'the Great Barber Case', the Government still has Charles Barber's money, now worth a considerable fortune.

The spelling takes the form of Barber, Berber, Barbor, Barbur, and Barbour; but in all cases the pronunciation was the same. The family was settled in the villages in the Peak district. We find them at *Chapel-en-le-Frith* (a 'frith' is a clearing in the forest), Chinley, Tideswell, Malcoff, Edale, Eyam, Hope Norton, Barber Booth, Hathersage, and down at Castle Donnington in south Derbyshire. An early mention of the name is a record of Richard le Barbut, of Brocton, a small hamlet in the wilds of the Peak. It was in the year 1283. Others are found at Glossop at the Darley Dale, where the Rev. John Barber was rector in 1382. In the fifteenth century we find one of the family trekking northward and settling in the wilds of Yorkshire at the village of Doncaster, where there is an old church containing a vault, and on the ancient tombstone is inscribed:

Sometime Honourable Merchant of Doncaster with Isabel and Rose, his two wives, which William dyed A.D. MCCCCXX whose souls by Mercy of Jesus Christ; Rest in Peace; Amen.

Ivan was born in Somerset East in 1892 and having completed his schooling in Grahamstown, joined his parents who had moved to Kenya and established a coffee farm at Kyambu outside Nairobi, having sold their lucerne farm in Potchefstroom the previous year. His father, Hal, had changed his name to Mitford-Barberton for reasons never fully explained.

At the outbreak of WW1, Ivan joined the East African forces operating against German East Africa in the vicinity of Kilimanjaro. Understanding ox-transport and being able to speak Ki-Swahili, he served with the Transport Corps which supplied the needs of the troops with seven convoys of 60 wagons each, mostly commandeered from the settlers. Ivan wrote: 'The roads were only tracks through the bush. There were no bridges, and in the heavy rainy season the mud was two feet deep. Owing to sniping and attacks by the enemy the transport was all done at night. Just imagine what a picnic it was to get sixty heavily laden wagons down into a river and up the steep bank on the other side, with thirty-two oxen floundering in the mud, breaking yokes and getting themselves entangled in the chains, extra drivers cracking their whips and encouraging the oxen by twisting their tails; all this going on in the dark and often in the rain with only a pale moon or a smoky lamp to guide you'.

During the latter part of the war he was appointed Interpreter at the prisoner-of-war camp in Dar-es-Salaam. When he was discharged he suffered so much from malaria that his father decided that he should go to South Africa for a holiday. He remained in Grahamstown for medical treatment, and as a diversion joined the Grahamstown School of Art. The principal recognised Ivan's talents and encouraged him to make sculpture his profession.

Accordingly, he enrolled at the Royal College of Art in London and was awarded his ARCA degree. He spent a further year studying in Italy and France. On his return he was appointed lecturer in sculpture at the University's *Michaelis* School of Art. He served there for 24 years rising to principal.

He became well known as a sculptor and his work has been bought by leading galleries in South Africa. He has decorated many of the public buildings, including the South African *Mutual Life Assurance Building* in Cape Town, which has a carved granite frieze 120m long and also nine granite figures of native types, each 4m high and weighing three tons. This took four years to complete and was his biggest commission.

Higher up on the building are heads of an elephant and a baboon each nearly 3m high. He carved a large oak coat-of-arms of the Republic in the Senate, Cape Town, and another for the High Court in Pietermaritzburg. In the National Gallery, Cape Town, he carved nine teak panels depicting life at the Cape in the early days. For the Tongaat Sugar Company, he did three large architectural panels in cement and five bronze fountain figures and an elephant in fibre-glass. At the *Children's Red Cross Hospital* in Rondebosch there is a small bronze Peter Pan. Letter-carving is a speciality and may be seen in several memorials including the *University of Cape Town, Diocesan College, St Cyprians* and several churches. He held a number of one-man shows in Cape Town and overseas. Examples of his work are in art galleries in Cape Town, Grahamstown and Durban.

On the rocks at the base of Chapman's Peak, about 3m above sea level you will see the Hout Bay Leopard, a 1,4 m high, time-tarnished bronze statue created by Ivan whose studio used to be in the village. Some say this is the guardian of Hout Bay. It's a tribute to the many leopards which used to prowl the mountains and valleys of the area, the last one sighted was in 1930. The leopard was positioned there in 1963, as a gift to the people of Hout Bay.

The statue of *Jock of the Bushveld*, the faithful dog of Percy Fitzpatrick by Ivan Mitford-Barberton was originally unveiled in Fitzpatrick Park by Mrs Mackie-Niven, the daughter of the late Percy Fitzpatrick and moved to its present position outside the town hall during Barberton's Centenary in 1984. It is fitting that this town was named after the Barber brothers, his father and uncle.

I recall Ivan once telling me that the only work that really paid for itself was a bust of *Richelieu* which he executed for a brandy company!

This statue of Jan Smuts in Cape Town, unveiled on January 26,1974, is located at the historic Slave Lodge on Adderley Street

Michaelis School of Art in Cape Town

Mitford-Barberton at work

The Hout Bay Leopard

Basotho married woman

Jock of the Bushveld

Ivan's Wolraad Woltemade statue was erected in honour of the man that saved 14 crew of a ship that was wrecked in Table Bay in 1773

16

The Atherstones

INVIA VIRTUTE PERVIA

The Atherstones and the Barbers go back a long time – over two centuries in fact – when Thomas Barber married Mary Atherstone in Nottingham. Then a hundred   years ago Hilton Hilton-Barber married Fanny Atherstone. The Atherstones spring from an old Warwickshire family and the village named after the family still exists. They claim descent from the Saxon Athelstan. Atherstone Priory is mentioned in the Domesday Book. Tradition says that the Atherstones were deprived of their title - Earls of Atherstone - and estates for some political reason and the family must have sunk for some time into poverty and obscurity. Atherstone Priory was transferred in 1464 to the Carthusian monks and after it fell into disrepair, Atherstone Hall was built from the ruins of the priory.

Forward to 1760 when Hugh Atherstone set up business as a dyer in Nottingham. He married Ann Green and they produced a family of 15. When he died in 1819 a newspaper recorded his passing with the following words:

> Of husbands he was the most tender; of parents the most affectionate; and of Christians the most exemplary; and long, very long will his afflicted family have to lament his loss. And not only his friends but thousands will do too. For him the hungry never asked and went away unsatisfied, nor was the beggar ever spurned from his door.

One of his daughters married Thomas Barber and one of his sons, Edwin, was a poet who received a grant of a hundred pounds a year from the Crown. Another son was Dr

Atherstone, born in Nottingham in 1791. He qualified as a doctor at Guy's or Middlesex Hospital where he was a surgeon and then returned to Nottingham. On 13 December 1811 he married Elizabeth Damant at St. James Church, Piccadilly. In her diary Elizabeth wrote:

> We moved to lodgings in John Street on 3rd November, and two days afterwards we had Mr Dunne and a friend of his, Mr Atherstone, to dine with us. Blessed was that day for in the latter I trust I have found a friend for life. My heart felt interested in him the first moment I saw him, for goodness was depicted in his ingenuous countenance, sensibility in his looks, words and actions, while his tenderness towards the dear children, was another claim to my regard.

After their marriage, John and Elizabeth lived in Nottingham where he had a medical practice until 1817 when he they decided to emigrate to the Cape. They embarked on the Uitenhage Packet with Elizabeth's youngest brother, Edward, with his bride of only a few months, Mary Atherstone, who was also a niece of Dr John's. But such a terrible gale sprang up in the Channel and they decided to disembark at Deal, which was just as well as the vessel was lost on her voyage. They settled at Stowey in Somerset where John practised for the next three years. Then his uncle, Captain John Damant, Commissary- General with the 48th Regiment of Lammas, Norfolk, which was sent to Port Elizabeth in 1817, came home with such glowing accounts of the climate and resources of the country that Dr Atherstone was again induced to venture on the voyage, shipping as surgeon to the good ship Ocean in 1820. They left England on New Year's Day 1820 accompanied by another vessel, *The Northampton*. The voyage lasted six months, on account of the two ships 'outspanning' at sundown and laying to lest they should miss each other in the morning. During the voyage, a strong gale blew the two ships together, their rigging becoming entangled and had to be cut apart. Further tragedy was narrowly averted when the Ocean was fired on by the Portuguese battery at Porto Praia while anchored off St Jago in the Cape Verde Islands. A cannon ball actually landed in Dr Atherstone's cabin. This was intended for an East Indiaman seen approaching the shore without permission. A graphic account of a similar voyage by a settler named John Mandy who recorded the following:

> The ship weighed anchor and sailed out of the harbour that evening. A day after leaving Gravesend it came on to blowing tremendously hard, the sea running mountains high. We could not weigh anchor till Sunday afternoon (three days later) when our troubles began, the sea breaking over us in all directions - tables, chairs, boxes, plates and dishes, men, women and children all mixed together, tumbling over one another and all dreadfully sick. In the midst of this, the sea broke into our cabin windows, dashed glass and foam in, the things that were below rolling and sliding took to swimming.
>
> The passengers are composed of all classes, high and low, many of them becoming travellers for the first time in their lives. The wealthier families, who are not travelling on state assistance, have brought wagons and ploughs, huge chests of belongings which were piled into the hold to await the inevitable damage by the movement of the ship and the flooding of water.

Lucky appeared the ordinary class of emigrant who, having but a single chest, could sit upon it at his ease. However, the men of means had some compensation. At one of the ports, for an old coat I bought 200 oranges, a fine goat and kid and 13 coconuts. The children were never better in health and spirits. The family has had fresh beef ever since we left St Jago. They brought six bullocks on board which were devoured within the fortnight. I bought a fine sheep for a dollar and a turkey of 14 lb for an old pair of shoes. Our goat gave milk for tea night and morning.

Dr Atherstone was appointed District Surgeon of Uitenhage and in 1823 accepted a practice in Cape Town. His interests extended well beyond the medical profession. He was elected to the committee for the improvement of Cape wines and he wrote to the Secretary of State for the Colonies, Lord Henry Bathurst, proposing the establishment of a Public School of Natural and Experimental Philosophy and Chemistry. Dr Atherstone had already given lectures on the subject. He also solicited the support of Lord Charles Somerset (Governor of the Cape), whom he invited to sit for his brother-in-law, Thomas Barber, for a portrait to be hung in the new school.

In 1828 Dr Atherstone accepted the post of District Surgeon of Grahamstown replacing Dr Cowie, who had been bitten with the mania of exploring, which about this time seized upon the Albany traders. The Damant History says that he was:

The best of doctors and the handsomest of men. As clever as were his sons Dr Guybon Atherstone and Dr Edwin Atherstone, the Governor Somerset were never so loved as was the dashing sportsmanlike old man who found so much to enjoy in his long life and who probably cared little if his wife's relations regarded him as very selfish and not a little heartless.

Elizabeth died on 18 November 1838 and Dr Atherstone married Ann Damant, widow of Major TC White and niece of his first wife Elizabeth, on 20 August 1839. It seems that Ann continued to live at Table Farm and as her new husband had his practice to attend to, he probably spent part of his time there and the other at his house in Grahamstown.

In April 1855 Dr Atherstone was driving to the Convict Station near Howiesons Poort when the disselboom of his cart snapped and he was pitched forward on to the backs of the terrified horses. He managed to cling to the harness and gradually worked his way back into the cart. But his weight, he was a tall and heavily built man, tilted it backwards and he was thrown violently to the ground, sustaining severe injuries. He was quickly taken to his lodgings in High Street, but at the age of 64 years, the shock was too great and he never recovered, dying a month later on 13 May.

Dr Atherstone was buried at Table Farm and large numbers of mourners, including the Lieut. Governor, attended the funeral of the popular and much respected doctor.

Hugh Atherstone and his wife Ann (by Thomas Barber)

Storm at Sea

Henry Bathhurst

Grahamstown in the early days

17

Thomas Barber

(1741–1883)

Thomas Barber was a portrait painter of such esteem that in 1873, 50 years after his death, an exhibition of his work was held in Nottingham Castle. He was a celebrated figure in the Midlands and he visited many of the mansions of the noble families in the area - the 7th Duke of Portland at Welbeck Abbey and the Duke of Newcastle at Clumber Park - to paint their portraits. A portrait of Mrs Siddons, exhibited at the Royal Academy, was executed for one hundred and fifty guineas, the highest commission the painter had ever received.

Sarah Siddons (1755 –1831) was a British actress, the best-known tragedienne of the 18th century. She was most famous for her portrayal of the Shakespearean character, Lady Macbeth. Apart from his portraits, Barber was a landscape painter in the style of Constable. He twice refused a knighthood and, more significantly declined admission to the Royal Academy which required him to reside in London, preferring as he did the more rural existence of the Midlands. .

David Love (1750-1827) peddler-poet who kept a bookseller's shop, sold quack medicines, was occasionally locked up for his nomadic practices, and made a livelihood by his rhymes, acristics and hymns, which he sold for a half penny.

Cornelius Smelt (1748-1832) was an administrator who served as Lieutenant Governor of the Isle of Man from 1805 until his death in 1832. During Smelt's lifetime, a fund was raised for a portrait to be painted of the Lieutenant Governor; Smelt was against the idea, but it was painted by Thomas Barber in 1826.

General Sir George Anson, GCB, KTS (1769-1849) commanded a British cavalry brigade under the Duke of Wellington during the Peninsula War and sat for many years as a Member of Parliament. He was also a Groom of the Bedchamber to Prince Albert from 1836 to September 1841. In 1849 he was appointed governor of the Royal Hospital, Chelsea.

Benjamin Mayo (1779 –1843) The Old General James Montgomery (1771 – 1854), was a British editor, hymn-writer and poet. He was associated with humanitarian causes such as the campaigns to abolish slavery and to end the exploitation of child chimney sweeps. He published a A Selection of Psalms and Hymns adapted to the Services of the Church of England in 1810.

His wife Mary Atherstone is from an old Warwickshire family descended from the Saxon Athelstan

David Love

Cornelius Smelt

General Sir George Anson

Benjamin Mayo (The Old General)

James Montgomery

View over Nottingham Park with Lenton Priory in the distance. Lenton Priory was a Cluniac monastic house founded by William Peveral in the early 12th Century.

Trent at Wilford. The dense woodlands and picturesque river views made Wilford a popular retreat for many Nottingham people.

18

Miles Bowker

(1764–1838)

Miles Bowker brought out a large party with the 1820 Settlers, having been a successful sheep farmer in the Cheviots before emigrating. Miles and Anna Maria Bowker came from Gateshead, Northumberland, where Miles was a well-to do sheep farmer. He and his wife decided to emigrate in order to provide better opportunities for their large family of nine sons and a daughter. The main Bowker farm, Tharfield, was named after the farm owned by the family in England for almost 100 years. Over over 2 000ha in extent, it lay between two rivers, with three km of sea frontage.

Unlike the majority of other parties who generally banded themselves together, each paying their own share, Bowker's party for the most part consisted of his family, retainers and servants, all of whose passages he paid. His wife was the daughter of John Mitford of Mitford Castle in Northumberland. Miles married her when he was 44 and she was only 18. It is said that when he was a young man, he courted her mother. Her parents objected and he vowed that he would wait and marry her daughter. They left England in December 1799 and arrived at the Cape of Good Hope five months later, it took another three weeks before they reached Algoa Bay, now Port Elizabeth. The Settlers then had to travel another 130 miles overland before they reached the area in which they were to settle. Their youngest daughter Anna Maria Bowker was born in Table Bay while on their way to Algoa Bay.

Bowker was 75 when he died early in 1839 and is buried on Tharfield. By this time his four elder sons were already married and had farms of their own. They were all successful sheep farmers. His fourth son Holden inherited Tharfield.

Ivan Mitford Barberton's book, The Bowkers of Tharfield, describes the house:

Just in front of Bertram's House at 'Tharfield' is the old family graveyard. Originally this was old Miles Bowker's garden. He was buried here in 1839, in the place where he had spent so much of his old age tending his flowers and planting aloes and orchids collected from Tharfield bush. His sons took a span of oxen and pulled up a large stone out of the river and set it up as a headstone over his grave. As time went by, three other Bowkers were buried in grandfather's garden, and it is now recognized as the old Bowker cemetery. Some years ago we collected some money from the Bowker and set up a stone memorial carved with the Bourchier arms and the names of those buried there. The bush stones are too hard to carve; and they are not even numbered as they should be, to correspond with the names and numbers on the memorial. The tallest stone is that of Thomas Holden Bowker, and the pointed stone beside him marks the grave of his wife, Julia Eliza. Old Miles the Settler's gravestone is the second highest and next to him is the grave of his wife, Anna Maria (nee Mitford)'.

One of the Bowker sons recalled that the river mouth closed up altogether for a couple of months as a result of a serious drought. The remaining water became thick with fish and the natives could catch as many as they wanted without trouble. He remembered an old red milk wood tree with a stone embedded in its trunk:

When I was a little boy I used to pretend that it was a precious jewel known only to me - and the monkeys. There was always a troop of monkeys climbing about in the foliage up there. And those beautiful purple crested louries, exquisite birds.

Then there was the saga of the Bowker treasure. Old Miles Bowker and six of his sons were sitting down to their evening meal when news came of the invasion of the Xhosas from across the Fish River. The family treasures - willow-pattern plates, silver candelabras and many other heirlooms they had collected over the years, were piled on to the table and tied up in the table-cloth. Four of the Bowker brothers loaded the bundle on to a hand cart and struggled off into the darkness. After several hundred yards, they took a path off into some thick bush and by chance came across a huge antbear hole. The booty was lowered in, still wrapped in the huge tablecloth, and they filled in the hole with earth. As they finished heaping soil into the hole, the rain began to fall. They did not retrace their steps along the path but ran directly back home. After the war, they sought the hiding place but to no avail. The treasure has never been found although successive generations of Bowkers have dug at every likely spot in the valley behind the house.

Miles Bowker had an almost obsessive determination to create an environment in their new country that would mirror the finest characteristics of England. He was convinced that to be born British was to win first prize in the lottery of life, that Britain was superior to all other countries. To him, merely being British was in itself a true vocation. His earliest indoctrination at the public school he had attended had shaped his attitudes and behaviour. A man was taught to be disciplined, tough, uncomplaining, reserved, good in a team and acclimatized to order. In his philosophy of life, there was no place for any thought of wickedness. He was proud of his heritage; he meant no harm except to evil enemies, and in principle he wished the poor benighted natives nothing but well. Even from the far reaches of Africa, he still regarded the power of the British Throne with almost a superstitious veneration.

Bowker was rightfully one of the leaders of the community. Several other farming families had settled nearby. The original encampment, which had consisted of a number of huts around a long narrow low ceilinged barn, had been transformed into the thriving village of Bathurst, with some two dozen substantial houses, each with its own garden and orchard. Further afield were the Boer stock farmers. According to long established practice, they drove their flocks and herds onto unoccupied land during the winter months when grazing was depleted in the more settled areas. Some of them built primitive houses and became permanent dwellers. The few Boers that were accepted as house guests at Tharfield, while openly hostile to anything British, secretly admired many of Bowker's sentiments. To them he seemed to demonstrate an unshakeable patriotism which was not unlike their own. On his side, he never underestimated the strength and determination of the Boers. He regarded them in many ways as an African tribe, one that had coalesced from that community of mixed Dutch, Flemish, German and Huguenot stock which had originally settled in the Cape under the Dutch flag. Tight-knit, traditionalist, racialist, individualist, devout in a severe Calvinist style, the Volk were fundamentalists in life as in faith. They were suspicious of all change, determined to live by their own ideals, and convinced of their unalterable rights under a God of absolutes.

In a surprisingly short time since the arrival of the British settlers in the area, friendly relations were progressively established with their neighbours of Dutch origin. Intermarriages were not uncommon. Further equality flowed from the retrenchment of the infantry guarding the eastern frontier by order of the Secretary of State in England. Soon the British settlers were placed on the same footing for military purposes as the earlier Dutch colonists. The commando system, unique to South Africa, had been originally developed by the East India Company whereby a troop of soldiers would be reinforced by a strong party of armed farmers whenever a military presence was required. And this system was to be tested to the extreme. The constant harassment by the black tribesmen and the inability of the authorities to control it was the main focal point of dissatisfaction and protest on the part of English settler and Boer burgher alike. The frequent attacks on their farms, the theft of their livestock and the deaths of their menfolk in the reprisal raids had filled the community with an overpowering fury and frustration. War was in the air and it was never far from the everyday lives of the Barbers.

Miles Bowker (bronze sculpture by Ivan Mitford-Barberton).   *Red milkwood (Sideroxylon inerme)*

19

Hugh Barber

(1799–1838)

Our first Barber ancestor to come to South Africa was the second son of Thomas and Mary, born on Christmas Day in 1779 in Nottingham. He was named after Hugh Atherstone, his maternal grandfather. Hugh was schooled at Eton and then studied languages in Geneva where he learnt to speak French and German fluently. He enrolled at a college in London to study chemistry after he returned from Geneva. It seemed a far cry from his literary and linguistic nature but his father had insisted that his sons should also have a practical side to their lives. During his studies he met his future wife, Anna Hoare, the eldest child in the family of six. Her father, John Hoare, was the padre in Derby. Soon they were courting and after some months were engaged. She remained with her parents in Derby while Hugh completed his course and received a diploma. They had agreed that they should only marry once Hugh had secured employment, and this he managed to do, at a factory in Twickenham, Middlesex.

They were married at All Saints' Church in Derby in September 1829 and set off thereafter for a short honeymoon on the Continent. They lived in Twickenham for the first six years of their married life and during that period five children were born. But times were never easy. They realised that the salary Hugh earned was pitifully short of their requirements, and he supplemented his income by giving organ lessons and by playing in the local church on Sundays. Hugh's position with the company was not strong enough for him to secure an increase and their commitments were always beyond their income. He managed to get a better-paid job with a chemical company in Leamington, Warwickshire, but still he had to give music lessons and play in both church and chapel to make ends meet. It was in their new home that Frederick Guybon was born.

Meanwhile Frederick William Barber, Hugh's younger brother and third son of Thomas Barber the artist, emigrated to the Cape in December 1839 at the age of 26. As mentioned previously, he had completed his studies, also at Eton, and then went over to the Continent where he also studied analytical chemistry at the University of Heidelberg. At the same university their cousin William Guybon Atherstone was completing his medical degree before returning to Grahamstown to re-join his family. And so it was against this background that Fred wrote to his brother, urging him and his family to emigrate.

Thomas Barber assisted Hugh, Ann and the children with their fare and they secured a passage on barque *Susan* leaving Tilbury in June 1839. They were on the high seas for three months before they reached Algoa Bay. Port Elizabeth was now a flourishing commercial centre on the western shore of the bay. Substantial warehouses lined the main streets of the lower part of the town while neat residences stood on the high ground above where resided many settlers who, unable to make a living out of farming, had now become merchants, among the most enterprising in the Colony.

Hugh's brother Fred was there to meet them. Rather than journeying by road, he had arranged berths for them on a new steamer, *Sir John St Aubyn*, for the final stage of the journey to their new home in lower Albany. The *Sir John* had begun a regular service linking Table Bay and Algoa Bay with Port Frances on the mouth of the Kowie River.

Fred Barber accompanied his brother Hugh, Hugh's wife Anna and their five children to Port Frances where the mouth of the river had been narrowed by walls constructed of wattle logs banked behind with sand. The farm that Fred had secured for his brother was a portion of Oliveburn leased from the Bowker family. (Fred was courting the 22 year-old Bowker daughter, Mary Elizabeth.) The Barber family were enchanted with their new environment - even the wattle and mud hut which was their first habitation. It was shaded by a cluster of pomegranate trees and was situated on a grassy plain overlooking a valley running down to a river, steep-sided and wooded. The river opened out to form a large dam, the wall only recently having been completed. Game could be seen in the thickets of bush - duiker, dikkops and bush buck.

This was the first of many meetings between Hugh Barber and the Bowker family, and Hugh became particularly friendly with the two elder Bowker sons, William Monkhouse and Miles Brabbin.

When the War of the Axe broke out (see later chapter), Hugh, Anna and their children were living on a farm, Alston Fields in the Bedford District which was looted in the uprising. Soon after the birth of Frances Harriet, they lost their eldest son through illness. At this point, the fight seemed to go out of Hugh. After the funeral, the family heeded his decision to leave farming altogether and return to Grahamstown. They could not get a good price for the farm. Most of their cattle were never recovered. Hugh really suffered a huge blow to his fortunes as well as to his confidence. Although only 48, he was already an old man. He took a poorly paid job as organist at the Cathedral, also holding the post of librarian while Anna kept a school and cared for the family.

Later, when the children were grown up, Hugh and Anna moved to Cradock where they spent their remaining years. Hugh, according to Ivan Mitford-Barberton:

Represented the old type of English gentleman, a lovable character with the kindest of dispositions, refined manners and tastes. He played and sang well and was highly accomplished in many subjects, but unfortunately he was not a good businessman and had a hard struggle for existence in adverse circumstances, being also handicapped with the claims of a large family.

20

Fred Barber

(1813–1892)

Here I wish to record some of the adventures of Mary Elizabeth's two children, Frederick Hugh and Henry Mitford (the latter subsequently changed his name to Mitford-Barberton). The founding of Barberton in the Eastern Transvaal in 1884 is officially attributed to Graham Barber although it could just as well be his cousins Fred and Hal in whose company he proceeded to Moodie's farm in the De Kaap valley in February 1884 Moodie was the surveyor-general of Transvaal who was given the farm as a reward for his services in surveying the railway line from Lourenco Marques to Pretoria.

In the museum in Barberton is a document narrated by Henry (Hal) Barber some 30 years after the time and hitherto unpublished, which sheds light on the early days of gold prospecting in that area. In 1884 Hal and his brother, Frederick Hugh Barber, were farming cattle and ostriches on the farm Broxley, 12 miles west of Grahamstown. One day there appeared in the newspapers a paragraph about gold being discovered in the de Kaap valley. Graham Hoare Barber, who was visiting the Cape from England, wrote from Port Elizabeth suggesting that if the news were true, they should be 'in it'.

To finance the excursion, Fred and Hal decided to sell their farm, the buyers being Dr Edwin and Charles Atherstone. Within a week, the party, accompanied by Edward White, son of George White of Braak Kloof farm, set off for Port Elizabeth, where they were joined by Graham Barber. They embarked on a small steamer, the Dunkeld, bound for Natal, spending the unusually rough voyage in the smoking room as the cabins were small and stuffy. In Port Natal they spent a few days with Colonel Bowker, Hal's uncle, before moving on to Pietermaritzburg:

There they spent a week buying wagons and oxen and two scotch carts and picks and shovels and lots of necessaries for gold digging, and fitting out generally for the coming trip. They also acquired a large marquee tent, nice dogs and good horses, with plenty of guns and cartridges, fishing rods etc.

The party travelled by train from Pietermaritzburg via Langsnek where they visited the battlefields of the first Anglo-Boer war - Ingogo, Majuba and Langsnek, to Lake Chrissie in the Transvaal. An eccentric Scotsman, Alexander McCorkindale, was responsible for the name Lake Chrissie. He fell in love with this area which reminded him so much of his home country, Scotland, and he bought 200 farms from the ZAR government to establish an immigration scheme. He and his wife did not have children and were very fond of Christina Pretorius, President MW Pretorius's daughter. They renamed Zeekoei pan, as it was then called, to Miss Chrissies lake, which later became Chrissiesmeer.

The Barber party took the opportunity of some hunting - *round the lake were a great many duck, spurwing geese, widgeon, teal and the large Egyptian geese.* Here, at the Simmer & Jack mine stores, they met up with Mr Jack which stood them in good stead in later years in the floatation of the Simmer & Jack gold mine on the Witwatersrand.

They also met up with their old friend Sprainger, an old hunting companion from their trip to Matabeleland in 1878, and Henry Nourse who was going up to the goldfields as Moodie's agent, as the Pioneer Reef had been discovered on Moodie's farm.

According to Hans Bornman, who wrote a history of the area:

Moodie engaged the help of Henry Nourse to discuss and negotiate matters with the prospectors. Nourse met Graham Barber and his two cousins Fred and Harry Barber on his journey at Chrissiesmeer and prevailed upon them to accompany him to Moodies as he expected trouble. Fortunately Nourse could persuade the diggers to listen to his proposals and he and his companions joined in the search for gold. David Wilson was appointed the new Gold Commissioner in January 1884 and in May of the same year took up his post at Kaapsche Hoop. The diggers were still unruly and his duty was to restrain them and restore law and order.

George Piggott Moodie had obtained a concession from the Republican Government to build a railway line from Klipstapel, near Lake Chrissie, to the Portuguese border. Although the project was never commenced, Moodie was granted 12 farms in the Barberton area. Then he heard that gold had been discovered on his property by Auguste Robert, known as French Bob. Moodie offered French Bob and his prospecting party the right to work their claims for 18 months only. He offered all other diggers extortionate terms of 50% of all net profits in exchange for working rights to claims, resigned his Government position and set off for England to float a company to exploit his discoveries. The diggers wanted the new gold area to be declared a public digging with a mining commissioner appointed by the Government to register claims and control the field. At this stage there were some 500 prospectors, all highly incensed towards Moodie. Henry Nourse, a big strapping fellow, was nevertheless extremely nervous of his reception by the diggers; hence his relief at meeting the Barbers.

Moodie, meanwhile, on his journey to England had got as far as Pietermaritzburg where he met a group of financiers, including Theophilus Shepstone who persuaded him to float a purely South African company. They offered him 20 000 pounds sterling for a half share in all his Kaap Valley farms which Moodie accepted with alacrity and the Moodie's Gold Mining & Exploration Company was formed. They got a court order against the diggers occupying the Moodie farms but, in a spirit of co-operation, replaced the original demand of 50% of profits with a 15% levy. But the miners refused and left the area in search of gold reefs in the neighbourhood.

The Barber party, which included Holden Bowker and Edward White, completed their onerous journey to the de Kaap valley. The roads were non-existent, nothing more than a few wheel tracks. When they arrived, they found that the diggers had formed a committee of nine members under the chairmanship of Harry Culverwell. However, they were not hostile to the newcomers - in fact seemed to get on quite well with them. The Barbers left Nourse and started prospecting on their own. In June 1884, they stumbled across an isolated narrow little creek with quartz deposits. They crushed and panned the ore in the little stream running through the ravine, and could hardly believe the results. They immediately pegged the reef at the foot of the hill in the name of Barber's Reef. The news of the discovery brought a great influx of diggers. Other reefs were found, including the famous Sheba, the Kimberley Imperial and others. Canteens, restaurants, shops and a post office sprang up like mushrooms on the quiet veld. The spot where their base camp was pitched in the valley ultimately became the town of Barberton.

The Transvaal Mining Commissioner, who had come to establish some sort of Government control, officiated at the christening ceremony. This was marked with the swilling of a good deal of Portuguese gin, the consumption of Swazi tobacco, much noise and good fellowship. A committee was elected consisting of Messrs Eade, Rhino Otto, S Wright, and Fred and Hal Barber.

There followed a gold rush including many prospectors from the Sabie and Pilgrim's Rest area where the alluvial gold had been exhausted. The diggings also attracted fortune seekers from many parts of the world as well as investors, the majority of whom lost everything through over-speculation in undeveloped companies. Barberton nevertheless enjoyed a spectacular boom. According to the noted South African writer TV Bulpin:

The streets were crowded with some of the most picturesque characters ever know in Southern Africa. Weather-battered prospectors such as French Bob; immaculately dressed company promoters such as the dapper little Alfred Beit; gamblers such as Ikey Sonnenberg; racing men such as Ramsay Macnab, all busy promoting schemes calculated to win them riches beyond belief. Footpads and highwaymen lurked round the fringes of society and at the height of the frenzy the local newspapers regularly published what they called 'murder and outrage' columns. Two stock exchanges did a roaring business night and day; (these were the first institutions of their kind in the southern hemisphere) while dozens of canteens, grog shops, bars and music halls contended with the mines as the greatest money makers in the town. Reigning beauties such as Cockney Liz, Florrie and the Golden Dane put themselves up for auction in the evenings."

The *Barberton Herald* was founded in 1886, later amalgamating with the *Gold Fields News*, forerunner of the present *Lowveld Leader.*

The problem of supply was a serious one. One route was the wagon road to the railhead at Ladysmith in Natal. This was a long and arduous trek but comparatively safe. The other was the shorter but dangerous route to Lourenco Marques, a wagon road having been opened by the Portuguese. The Portuguese Government later granted a concession to build a railway between that town and the Transvaal border to an American citizen by the name of McMurdo. (Delagoa Bay was first occupied by the Portuguese as far back as 1721. The settlers established a fort and a trading station known as Fort Lagoa but after a few years the settlement was abandoned due to the prevalence of malaria.) President Paul Kruger followed this up by granting a railway monopoly to a Holland-German syndicate. Newmarch and Rimer formed a company to work the reef discovered by the Barbers at Rimers Creek (still known by that name). They erected a ten-stamp battery and the first 100 tons of ore yielded 5 ounces to the ton. The property was amalgamated with the great Sheba mine which together with Bray's Golden Quarry, yielded 50 000 ounces of gold from the first 13 000 tons milled.

Meanwhile the Barber brothers had returned to the Eastern Cape where they farmed ostriches at Junction Drift on the Fish River. However, news of the discovery of gold on the Witwatersrand drew them back and they settled at Ferreira's Camp. Fred Barber floated the Ferreira into a company, and he and Hal acted as promoters and directors of many other companies. They were both directors of the Transvaal and Delagoa Bay Investment Company and Fred a director of the Johannesburg Board of Executors. However, such was the fragility of their business interests that, following a visit to England and Europe, they returned to find their fortunes had crashed. They had to liquidate most of their holdings to pay off their debts and their cousin Hilton had to lend them 500 pounds to get them back on their feet again.

It was not long before the prospect of hunting lured them back from their more ordered farming lives. In 1877 the two brothers, equipped with a wagon, oxen and a quantity of trade goods, travelled to Bechuanaland, where they were received by Paramount Chief Khama at Bamangwato. They asked his permission to capture wild ostrich chicks at Lake Ngami but this was not forthcoming. So they pressed on northwards. They visited the ancient gold mines of the Tati and 'Blue Jacket' which were in the process of being opened up. There they ran into Selous on one of his hunting trips. They camped at Makobie's Kopje while runners were sent on to obtain Lobengula's permission to enter Matabeleland, and when this was granted, trekked on to Bulawayo. They were granted an audience with the king at Matjeumhlope.

On hearing their request to shoot elephants, Lobengula directed them to a camping site on the outskirts of Bulawayo where several other parties of hunters and traders were already ensconced. They often visited the king, who was very friendly towards them. On one occasion he invited them to dinner which consisted of meat and 'tshwala' (beer) served in such great quantities that it took them days to recover. Fred Barber, following the accepted procedure of calling on the King wherever he happened to be at the time, reporting themselves, exchanging civilities and presents, eating fat meat, drinking beer and making friends. Barber recorded his impressions of the royal court:

> We were told that 'Loben' was down in his lands supervising his many spouses and slaves, who were preparing the soil for the next season's mealie crops. Proceeding thither, we espied the burly potentate sitting on the top of a small rocky eminence, while below and about him, perched upon their hams, were about forty majakas (young soldiers), his bodyguard. It was evident that the King was in good humour, as they were chattering and laughing and noisily discoursing. Below them in the fields, a considerable number of women and slaves were cultivating the soil with hoes.

Lobengula joked about his name: *"You say your name is Barber? Why, that's my name."* ('Baba', signifying 'Father' was the name by which he was addressed by his people.)

> He asked us all about our journey, and whether our oxen were healthy and not affected with any contagious diseases. What was the object of our journey? Were we hunters or traders? And he chaffingly asked us if we were not frightened to go into the hunting country, as lions and elephants were dangerous things to shoot.

After a while, he invited his visitors to the kraal to drink beer and have something to eat:

> As he strode along, followed by his shouting and singing *majakas*, we could not but admire his jaunty and dignified carriage, powerful build, and massive limbs. Around his waist was a great apron of cat and monkey tails, completely encircling his loins. Bar sunshine, a few ivory rings and brass armlets were his only attire. His hair was worked up to an apex, surrounded on the top by an oily shining ring, or s*ekethla*. His face was pleasant in conversation, with a humorous twinkle in his eye. He was ready-witted and loved a joke, a grand savage, and every inch a king, a fit ruler for the savage hordes over whom he had to wield a firm and stern sway. Arriving at the kraal, he climbed upon his wagon and perched himself on the front wagon box, while we found sitting places where we could, on the wagon pole and stumps of trees forming the kraal. Gradually the kraal filled with *indunas*, headmen, and followers. Maidens handed round *Buchala* beer in closely woven baskets. A have no doubt but that he thought he was paying us a delicate compliment. Had it not been for the great respect, if not awe, with which we regarded him, we should have burst into laughter, but he was not a man to be laughed at, ridiculous though he make himself.
>
> We sat him down on our strongest chair and contemplated him nervously, lest he should go through it, and were greatly relieved when it held. We produced a bottle of French brandy, and had to sip some from his glass to show that it was not poisoned. Then we drank to our better acquaintance. Then we chatted and brought out and showed

him our elephant guns and had some rifle practice with them. My brother and I gave him a silver- mounted revolver and a silver mug with a glass bottom. He was delighted with both, especially the mug, which he hugged and carried away in his hand and used all the time we were there, and was still using on our return from the hunting country.

Beer, in a big vessel was handed to us, to which we did ample justice. The King's beer was always good! Then followed a huge flat-bottomed wooden dish with a savory joint of beef. The King cut this into chunks as big as a leg of mutton, using his left hand as a fork. A chunk was handed us. We pulled out our pocket knives and hacked it up and 'chawed'. It was splendidly cooked, we were hungry, and hearty old hunters found no difficulty in dining in this primitive manner, and in no time our hunger was appeased.

Next morning after breakfast an extraordinary apparition approached our wagons. It was some time before we could analyse it. We thought it was some new arrival, some gigantic Dutch-man bound for the bush veld. It stalked into our bush fence round our wagons. *Lobengulo! Lo and behold! What a metamorphosis!* The cat and monkey tails had given place to a complete suit of brown moleskin, his huge limbs and feet were encased in Wellington boots, and a spreading brown wide-awake felt hat covered his sable brow. It was absurd, ridiculous. Loben in European clothes was no longer a king, the dignity of his savage majesty had gone. He was no longer picturesque, but he was quite satisfied with himself.

Finally, the king's approval for hunting elephants was given. It was customary for a present to be given for this concession. They set out north, past Umgeni and established a base camp at Linkwasi. Here they met up with Fred and Spencer Drake amongst other hunters. (The Drake family now lives near us in Tzaneen and Spencer Junior farms timber and avocados)

In 1894, at the age of 44, Hal married Mary Layard Bowker, third daughter of Thomas Holden Bowker of Tharfield. This branch of the family finally moved to Kenya where they farmed in the Eldoret district until they died within a year of each other. In the cemetery there is a massive stone tomb erected over their graves, the inscription of which reads:

These hardy pioneers blazed many a trail into the wilds: They were brave hunters and friends of all men. They founded Barberton in 1884 and were leading pioneers in Kimberley and Johannesburg. England were not England were her sons other than these.

Fred's diaries were annotated by Edward C Tabler

Flamingos on Lake Chrissie

Auguste Robert

Theophilus Shepstone

Sheba mine is one of the few which is still being mined today

An early photograph of Rimer's Creek

Cockney Liz

King Lobengula

Lobengula's youngest daughter

Fred's diaries were annotated by Edward C Tabler

Matabele warriors

Buffalo about to charge

21

Hilton Barber

(1842–1928)

My paternal **great grandfather, Hilton,** the first of the line to be born in South Africa, was the seventh and last but one child of Hugh and Anna Barber. He was born on George Cumming's farm Hilton just outside Grahamstown on the last day of February in 1842. On his death on 6 September 1928, the following obituary notice (couched in some-what extravagant language which has imbued in his progeny an inflated but excusable sense of pride) appeared in a local newspaper under the heading 'Horse-Breeder and Sportsman':

Death yesterday morning removed from our midst at the age of 86 Mr Hilton-Barber, a South African gentleman, widely-known, popular and much-respected throughout this country and who's passing away at so ripe an age will be universally lamented.

Mr Hilton-Barber, during the earlier years of his career, lived in British Kaffraria, where he carried on merino sheep-farming until in 1875 he moved into the Midlands, having bought from Mr Thomas Scanlon the farm which has now become so well known, Hales Owen, near Cradock, where he lived for over half a century and has died there. His coming to the Cradock district synchronised with the meteoric rise in the ostrich-farming industry, into which Mr Barber plunged with all his natural foresight and energy and in which he rapidly reached the highest pinnacle of success as an ostrich breeder. At the same time being an ardent admirer of what to him was a noble creature, a good horse, he laid the foundation of the famous Hales Owen Thoroughbred Stud. Instinctively an unerring judge of a good animal, he spared no expense in keeping up his stud to the highest standard in well-selected sires and mares and established and maintained to the last a reputation of being in the foremost ranks of the thoroughbred breeder.

Only recently it will be remembered when his age and health no longer permitted him to give personal attention to his stud, did he dispose of it by public auction.

Every inch a sportsman of the first water, he indulged during the greater portion of his life in the *Sport of Kings*', and only until a short while ago, Mr Hilton Barber, stately in figure, handsome, and with an attractive personality, was one of the most heartily-welcomed visitors on the course.

All who knew him also knew what he meant to horse racing, for it was his ambition to hold high the tone of that noble sport, and indeed by few men have its traditions as a clean and honourable pastime been maintained with greater sincerity. The incentive to the pursuit of high-class horse breeding in this country has in a greater measure also been due to that princely sportsman, Mr Hilton Barber.

While Hilton was at school in Grahamstown, he spent his holidays with his uncle Fred Barber and his remarkable aunt Mary. Uncle Fred had so much more spirit and determination than Hilton's father Hugh who was more suited to playing an organ in the church than coping with the rough and tumble of a farmer's life. Fred too, found the young Hilton a lively and stimulating young man and unofficially 'adopted' him. Hilton was five years' older than Fred's own firstborn and filled the role of an elder son. Fred Barber still maintained close contact with his cousin William Guybon Atherstone, in whose company he had come out to the Cape, and his uncle, Dr John Atherstone, Guybon's father. Dr John had relinquished his medical calling - he had been district surgeon of Grahamstown for as long as anyone could remember - and was now farming full-time at Iron Pot. His first wife Elizabeth, whom he had married in England before emigrating and with whom he had eight children, died in the 1830s. In 1942 Dr John married again, to Ann, the widow of Major Thomas Charles White and a niece of his first wife.

Hilton often accompanied his uncle Fred on visits to the Atherstones and it was on one of the visits to Iron Pot that he met Fanny Atherstone, a lovely daughter by this second marriage, with whom he fell in love and was to marry four years later.

By the time Hilton was 20, he moved permanently to his Uncle Fred's farm Highlands where he wanted to learn everything he could about sheep farming. However, Highlands was hardly the ideal sheep farm situated as it was in Upper Albany, in wild and stony country with great woods and deep valleys. In those days it was more of a paradise for sportsman and naturalist. Game was plentiful and there was much undiscovered in its flora and fauna which was eminently suited to the tastes of Fred and Mary Elizabeth. It was not long, therefore, before Hilton accepted an offer from Tom White (senior) to take over a section of Gray Park near King William's Town. Mr White, showing a remarkable confidence in the young man's potential, generously gave him 1 500 sheep on 'tick'. This confidence was born out for within a few years Hilton was so successful that he was able not only to purchase the farm but also to return the sheep.

It was still many years before wool farming on a large scale was properly established. But Hilton was in the forefront of the campaign which finally brought the farming of high quality sheep for wool into its own in this part of the country. Later, when Hilton was married and the proud father of five fine children, he decided that the Cradock area some hundred miles inland would be better suited to sheep rearing. He sold Gray Park for a handsome sum and was able to acquire Halesowen from a Mr Thomas Scanlon. In 1875, the year he moved his flocks to their new farm, he was clipping 10 000 pounds of high grade wool at every shearing from choice rams and ewes imported from Saxony.

At the age of 24, as predicted, he married Fanny, daughter of Dr John Atherstone of 'Iron Pot' near Grahamstown. They had a family of five sons and five daughters which firmly established the Barber clan in South Africa.

Hilton's passion for hunting was influenced no doubt by his Uncle Fred's quest for adventure beyond the borders of the Cape. The country north of the Orange, up to the Limpopo attracted big game hunters. Here the plains were stocked with immense herds of blue wildebeest and zebra whilst in the woodlands roamed large game such as buffalo, giraffe, sable and roan antelope, tsessebe, kudu and waterbuck. Frederick Courtney Selous, a legendary figure in the annals of exploration and hunting, and a companion to Theodore Roosevelt on safaris to several continents of the world, was a regular visitor to these areas. Hilton's first proper hunting trip came about through an invitation from his brother Graham, seven years his senior, and George Cumming, on whose farm he had been born 32 years ago, to join them in Pretoria for a six month hunt in 1874. Hilton was very serious about the logistics of the trip from King William's Town, through the Free State and up to the Transvaal. He obtained a small wagon and fitted it up comfortably with a cartel.

An account of his trip is recorded in his journal:

I had 10 beautiful Zulu cattle all alike in colour. I took one riding horse, and with a driver and leader, I started off. I got a sporting Snyder, a combination with 14-bore shot barrel and a double-barrel pin-fire 12-bore rifle. I travelled up in the wagon to the Transvaal which took many weeks. On the way, in the Free State, I had grand sport after wildebeest, blesbok and springbok. One morning, a little north of Bethlehem, I came across a large camp of trek Boers from the Western Province, on their way to the Transvaal. They were preparing for a big shoot on the adjacent flats. My horse was very tired and I told them that if they could give me a mount they could have my bag. We started off with a Scotch cart for the game, which I managed to fill myself with five wildebeest and two blesbok.

Hilton met up with his brother Graham and George Cumming in Pretoria as arranged. Then they set off to Lydenburg, then called Nazareth, and up the mountains toward Mac Mac – *'the roads were so bad that we had to reim three wheels of each wagon besides tying a mimosa tree at the back'*. At Pilgrim's Rest they found six hundred alluvial gold diggers. Hilton commented:

'They all looked the colour of the yellow sand in which they were working. They seemed very cheerful.' Then he added laconically: 'I never heard that they had any luck.

During the months that followed, they hunted along the Sabie River and the Lebombo mountains (now part of the Kruger National Park) on the Mozambique border. They shot all kinds of big game to the delight of some 40 native followers (who were particularly fond of fat quagga). They had some fine adventures with buffalo and lion. On one occasion Graham and Hilton pursued two buffalo into thick bush. They released the dogs to follow the spoor.

We heard the dogs give tongue and the buffalo crashing through the bush. They broke cover 150 yards below us, with the dogs snapping at their heels. We dismounted and fired. The bull was slightly wounded and we gave chase. It raced ahead and then hid behind some trees. We did not see it when we came up, and it charged. I fired at him when he was 15 yards from us. The bullet struck him a few inches too low on the forehead. As I pulled the trigger I jumped aside and the bull missed me by a few inches. Unfortunately, Hilton's horse which was standing nearby bore the brunt of the attack the buffalo's horns buried in its flank.

I only had time to take the saddle and bridle off my horse when he staggered and a bullet through the head finished poor old Foley, Hilton recorded.

Having shot all the game we cared to, we turned back to the place where we had left my wagon in charge of the driver. We found that lions had been there and killed two horses and several oxen. I told the driver and another man to show us where the lions had gone. We found five lions eating the carcase of an ox they had dragged off into the bush. The lions disappeared into a kloof. We followed the spoor and were able to bag three lionesses. We stayed there a week mending the wheel, which was no easy job. We drove half the spokes into the hub, the other half into the felloes and laced them together with raw buffalo hide.

The trip was a great success and Hilton never forgot the camaraderie and fellowship of the hunt. As Captain of Barber's Horse, Hilton served voluntarily in what was termed the Ninth Frontier War of 1877. This started as a feud between two factions of the Xhosa tribe-- the Galekas under Chief Kreli who occupied Galekaland, the territory between the Kei and Bashee Rivers, and the Fingos, who occupied the land west of the Kei. At this time there was a general feeling of uneasiness throughout the eastern frontier districts and the Fingo clans were stealing from the farmers on an unprecedented scale. The incident started after a wedding feast at a Fingo kraal just within the boundary. Late in the evening, when all were excited by dancing and beer drinking, a quarrel arose and one of the Galekas was killed. Three days later four large parties of Galekas, intending to avenge the insult offered to their friends, crossed the little stream that formed the boundary of Fingoland and captured 140 head of horned cattle and 600 sheep and goats. The acting resident, Mr West Fynn, proceeded immediately to the scene and pointed out to the Galekas that they were doing wrong. Chief Mapasa, whose retainers the raiders were, admitted that they were in fault and promised that the captured animals would be restored. However, some of the cattle had now been slaughtered at once and eaten, others had strayed away and could not be found. There followed a number of petty acts of hostility which resulted in 150 of the frontier armed and mounted police being sent across the Kei to guard the Fingo border and prevent raids from either side. However, the situation escalated. More raids took place accompanied by loss of life. More troops were brought in and a full-scale war developed between the two factions resulting in utter lawlessness in the area. The Galekas asserted that they were making war upon the Fingos only and had no wish to molest whites, but shortly after an army of 5 000 strong crossed the border and encountered the mounted police. Several battles ensued but the Galekas were not routed.

George McCall Theal, in his *History of South Africa* records the events thus:

The Governor of the Cape, Sir Bartle Frere, issued a proclamation formally deposing Chief Kreli of all his power and authority. This was without meaning for his tribesmen - no power but death could deprive him of the right to which he was born. Nevertheless it did mean that Kreli's country was taken away from him and was reserved for disposal from the imperial authorities and was to be ruled directly by officers appointed by the government of the Cape Colony. The country was totally unprepared for war but it was fortunate (for the colonial authorities) that there was a British regiment of the line to guard various positions of protection, and that the governor himself, two members of the ministry, and the general commanding the imperial troops happened all to be in King William's Town. The aim of the colonial forces was to break up the *Galeka* army, to destroy the kraals so that the fighting men could not rally again, and to capture the cattle in order to bring the people to submission.

(The cattle captured were to be distributed as prize).

It was not an easy task since the Galekas broke up into small parties. At this point the volunteer forces were brought into the fray as well – from Albany, Fort Beaufort, Cradock, Tarkastad, Wodehouse and Aliwal North. It is not clear whether their main motivation was the "prize" but it is recorded that, at the end of the hostilities, the Galeka division of the Xhosa tribe has ceased to exist as a community and about 13 000 head of horned cattle, a still greater number of sheep and goats, and several hundred horses had been taken from them – and some 700 of their warriors had been killed. The volunteers and burghers were received with much rejoicing as they passed through the villages and towns on their way back to their homes. (Thus Hilton Barber's service in the protection of his country can be seen in its proper perspective, not that this should detract from his good name.)

Getting back to farming matters, it was at Gray's Park that Hilton first interested himself in horse racing and his passion for racing was continued at *Hales Owen*. Among his most successful racers were *Billy, Gambush, Masher, Paramount and Oxygen*. *Oxygen* won the first South African Derby run on October 17 1895 at Port Elizabeth for a stake of four hundred pounds. Hilton was a patron of the turf in Cape Town (Kennilworth became the headquarters of the SA Turf Club in 1874), Uitenhage, Grahamstown, Graaff-Reinet and the Bay. In the 1885/86 season, *Oxygen* won over one thousand pounds in stake money and was by far the most successful horse on the circuit. Hilton's jockey, Curly Longhurst, rode in most of them. The farming folk and those from the nearby towns, attended these race meetings in full force, and the course often resembled laagers of other days. Apart from scores of races of less importance, he won seven South African Derbies, five of which were at Port Elizabeth, one in Johannesburg and one in Durban. He took the '92 Derby with *Foam* who frightened away all opposition bar three hopefuls. Ridden by Curly Longhurst, *Foam* started at 4 to 1 on and won as he liked.

In those early days Port Elizabeth was the racing capital of the Cape and the first totalisator was put into operation there in 1885. Business was booming and the harbour was busy with men and material bound for Kimberley. Then the Johannesburg Turf Club was formed in 1887 and the opening of the railway in 1893 meant that Hilton Barber, together with many VIPs from racing centres in other parts of the country, could attend the meetings and rub shoulders with the leading sportsmen of the Witwatersrand - George Farrar, Abe Bailey, Woolf Joel and AC Harris. In the course of his racing career, Hilton also came to know many important people, including Cecil Rhodes, Alexander Starr Jameson and Sir Hamilton Gould-Adams. When he visited England in 1880 in the company of his brother-in-law Frank Holland and George Armstrong, he purchased two famous racehorses as the foundation for his stud, *Buxton* (unbeaten in South Africa in his 15 starts) and *Earl Koenig*. Twenty years later, when he was in England again, this time accompanied by his third son Monty, he bought another clutch of good racehorses, *Cherry Ripe* (which was to win the two hundred pound stake at 5 to 1 at the first meeting at Milnerton Turf Club in 1908), *Sauce Tartar, Desert Maid, Lady Trenton* and *Admiral* (which was to win the Johannesburg Summer Handicap in 1910).

Hales Owen became a by-word in the racing fraternity, surpassed only as the principal breeding establishment by Henry Nourse's stud farm at Middelburg which had world recognition. Hilton was one of the fathers of the South African turf who raced for the love of racing. He was a founder member of the Thoroughbred Breeders Association together with Charles Southey, AL Robertson, A Forbes and EL Birch. He was a familiar figure in the district in his carriage and perfectly matched chestnut pair.

In 1882 Hilton's wife Fanny died and five years later he married Alice, daughter of Major Boys. Hilton's five elder children - Harry Atherstone, Sydney, Florence Grant, Hugh Montague and Mary Atherstone - were all born before the move to *Hales Owen*. (The boys all finished their education at St Andrew's College in Grahamstown). Five younger children - Ida Mildred, Ethel Atherstone, Charles Evelyn, Graham Atherstone and Fanny Atherstone - were born in Cradock. Charles had a playful streak and taught the family parrot to mimic his father's voice when he stood on the stoep and called out to his groom, Spandiel, to '*inspan* the carriage'. So successful was he that Spandiel frequently appeared at the front door with the horses *inspanned*, only to find that this order had come from the parrot!

Hilton soon acquired the reputation as the foremost ostrich breeder in the district. He was therefore the natural target for an enterprising *smous* who appeared one day at Hales Owen with a flock of footsore, thin and weary ostriches, offering them for sale. Hilton naturally turned him down. The *smous*, not in the least discouraged, then said he had a large sum of money on him, and as he did not like trekking around with it, asked Hilton if he would take it and give him a cheque. Hilton obliged. For the next few weeks, the *smous* visited all the farmers in the district, showing them Hilton's cheque, and saying that if wise old Mr Hilton-Barber had bought birds for that amount, he must have known they were good stock and only needed feeding. Needless to say, he sold every bird. Hilton was apparently livid when he heard how he had been used. On another occasion, one of his grandchildren recollected, an Afrikaans-speaking *smous* called at *Hales Owen* just as lunch was being served. Karoo hospitality being what it was, he was invited to share the meal. He remarked that he had already eaten, but would just have a *peusel* (nibble). He proceed to demolish a huge plateful and as he was leaving, Hilton told him that next time, he should please *peusel* at his home and eat here at *Hales Owen!*

Later in life Hilton compounded his two names into a surname, calling himself Hilton Hilton-Barber. It is not known why this was done but it might have had some connection with his cousin Hal Barber (favourite Uncle Fred's second son) changing his name to Mitford-Barberton. Both families henceforth assumed this double name.

And so, all Hilton-Barbers extant today are descended from Hilton, the 'laird' of *Hales Owen*. An incident showing what a well-respected, popular man Hilton was, occurred at the Port Elizabeth Show in 1925, when Admiral Goodenough, in charge of the South African Navy, was inspecting his troops. At the march-past, as a mark of respect, the Admiral asked Hilton to acknowledge the royal salute.

Curly Longhurst on Oxygen

Merino sheep

This fine painting of a quagga is by Nicholas Robert (1614-1685)

Paramount Chief Kreli
(Photo in the Grey Collection)

Sir Hamilton Gould-Adams, Lieut- Governor
of the Orange River Colony

Sir Bartle Frere

22

Morgan Williams

(1865–1908)

Morgan Williams was a medical doctor, a member of the Royal College of Surgeons and a specialist in tropical diseases. In 1895 Dr Williams answered an advertisement placed by the British South Africa Company for a position as Houseman at the Bulawayo Hospital. He arrived in Bulawayo the following July, having sailed to Cape Town, travelled by train to Mafeking and completed the final leg on horseback with the Second Pioneer Column. Upon his arrival, he found that the post had already been filled so he rode on to Salisbury. There Dr Andrew Fleming, Chief Medical Officer of Rhodesia, offered him the post of District Surgeon, with private practice, at Victoria (later known as Fort Victoria, and more latterly, Masvinga).

The Matabele Rebellion of July 1896 was in full swing and Morgan joined the Victoria Rifles Volunteer Force as Surgeon-Lieutenant. Besides being an amateur prospector on the Victoria Gold Fields, he was also a remarkably good shot, even in that era when so many men lived by the gun. He also had a reputation for being one of the kindest- hearted men in town.

Early in 1899, Morgan took the long journey back to Wales where he married Gertrude Bowen on 4 July at St Peter's Church, Llanelli. He was 33 and she was 21. Gertrude, the daughter of a well-to-do industrialist, had recently completed her education at Gorton College, Cambridge. Packing her worldly possessions in heavy trunks, she accompanied him back to Africa on the Kinfanns Castle's maiden voyage to Durban.

The Anglo-Boer War had broken out and Durban was a mass of soldiers. They travelled by train from Durban to Salisbury, by coach to Enkeldoorn and by ambulance to Victoria, by courtesy of the doctor. On the way, whilst fording a drift, Gertrude's cabin trunk of beautifully handmade blouses fell off the coach and vanished into the river, never to be seen again. She arrived with a trunk of skirts, with no tops to wear with them. From then on, she always mixed the clothes in every trunk she packed! Gertrude was immediately given the task of nursing a detachment of the Australian Imperial Regiment who had contracted typhoid. (This regiment was to assist Colonel Herbert Plumer, commander of the British military force in Rhodesia, in the relief of Mafeking in May 1900.)

In 1900 Gertrude gave birth to their first child, a daughter, whom they named Kathleen. However, within a few months she died. Three years later, on 20 November 1903, Gerwin David Bowen Williams was born.

An incident of historical interest took place in the early hours of Sunday, 20 February, 1904. The remains of Major Allan Wilson and his ill-fated comrades of the Shangani Patrol of 1894 were exhumed from their burial place. This was in accordance with the wishes of the late Cecil John Rhodes, as expressed in his Will, that they should be buried alongside Rhodes' Grave at World's View in the Matopos. The exhumation was officiated by Dr Morgan Williams along with the Magistrate and the Reverend Haliward.

The Shangani Patrol was a group of 34 members of the BSA police which fought over 3 000 Matabele just north of the Shangani River. They were part of Major Patrick Forbes' force attempting the capture of Lobengula. Led by Major Allan Wilson, the patrol crossed the Shangani late on 3 December 1893 to scout ahead of Forbes' main BSAP column, and was ambushed on the morning of 4 December by numerically-superior Matabele riflemen and warriors. After sending three of his 37 men back across the river to fetch reinforcements, Wilson was forced into a last stand against a host which outnumbered his patrol about a hundred-fold. The rising of the Shangani in flood made it impossible for Forbes to provide assistance, and the 34 soldiers fought to the last cartridge, killing over 10 times their own number, before they were annihilated.

In March 1908 disaster struck the household when Williams contracted fever. Dr Andrew Fleming came down especially from Salisbury to attend Morgan, but not even his administrations could save him. (A grand old doyen of the medical profession in Southern Rhodesia, Dr. Andrew Milroy Fleming, CMG., CBE., later Fleming-Bernard and Laird of Dunsinane, had been working at the Kimberley Hospital as resident surgeon and was there personally engaged by Rhodes for service in the Company's territory in 1894, On 7 April, Morgan Williams died of malarial meningitis and was buried in Victoria. Gertrude, who was again pregnant, left with her son as soon as she could, and returned to her father, Samuel Bowen, in Wales. Inez Hester Bowen Williams was born on 11 December of that year.

Gertrude decided to move to England and took up residence at Bexhill-on-Sea. She became the matron at a preparatory school there. In 1919 she met and married Walter Repon Spreckley. She continued with her philanthropic work and in 1929 she was awarded the Order of Mercy which was conferred upon her at Buckingham Palace by the Prince of Wales. Her son, named Gerwin, was educated at Epsom College, Surrey, (founded in 1853 as a boys' school to provide support for poor members of the medical profession such as pensioners and orphans), and Queen Elizabeth School in Cranbrooke. He was not a model scholar and was always in trouble, according to his family. As soon as he could, he left school and was apprenticed as a learner farmer in Kent.

At the age of 18, however, he decided to return to Rhodesia and his mother appointed Gordon Huntley of Fort Victoria as his guardian. But, in Gerwin's words, "I got waylaid in South Africa to attend agricultural college at Grootfontein (near Middelburg) in the Cape". Unbeknown to him, his guardianship at his enrolment had been removed from Gordon Huntley and given to the principal of Grootfontein, WR Thornton. At this time, Gerwin became the illegal but proud owner of a .38 revolver which was accidentally discharged when Gerwin fell off his bicycle. Firearms were prohibited at the College and he was accordingly expelled.

Thornton had some sympathy for his charge and gave him an introduction to Monty Hilton-Barber who was then farming at Atherstone. Bill, as he became known to all his friends, embarked on a number of years of carefree living. An Indian motor cycle and sidecar was his preferred mode of transport, even when courting. He became a legendary shot with his .38 special S&W revolver, once bagging a leaping mullet through the gills! On night hunts, he was quicker on the draw than the local jackal hunters with their shotguns. Bill subsequently bought Hilton South, a small farm adjoining Atherstone. It was when Hester came out from England to visit him that she met Tom, and they were married soon afterwards.

Gertrude Spreckley decided to immigrate to South Africa in the same year and bought the "Old Home", for many years the homestead of the Mullins family. This became the St Andrew's sanatorium (and later Graham House) and Gertrude moved to Langholme at 7 Worcester Street, making it into a gracious Edwardian home. "Spreckles", as she was affectionately known, served as President both of the Women's Auxiliary of the British Empire Services League and of the Settlers Club.

She enjoyed a further 30 years of active life in Grahamstown before she died on 18 February, 1962. Ronald Currie, past Headmaster of Michaelhouse and St Andrew's College, and a great personal friend, paid tribute to "Spreckles" in the Grocott's *Daily Mail*:

> Gertrude Spreckley has been described as an Edwardian; and this age was perhaps not altogether an Earthly Paradise in England. But there was about it graciousness and a great dignity and a goodness of heart; and it is these things which Gertrude Spreckley brought to us in Grahamstown.

Tom, apart from being a successful farmer, also established Coldsprings Dairy in Grahamstown and took a keen interest in local government. He was the youngest ever councillor elected to the Albany Divisional Council, which he served on until his death. Tom and Hester's first child, Shirley Atherstone was born on 21 February 1935. Their second daughter, Margaret, died in infancy. Tom was unable to serve in World War II due to 'petit mal' condition caused, it is said, by an accident at the age of nine when he was knocked down outside the Port Alfred railway station by a taxi owned by a Mr Cousins.

Hester was a great help to him on the farm, recording all the milk weights and collecting milk from other farms in the very early hours to supply Coldspring Dairy when their own milk was insufficient. At times she ran the dairy in town. Tom was tragically killed in a shooting accident on a neighbouring farm, Medbury, on 25 November 1945. Coldspring farm and all the cattle were sold, as was the dairy and Hester moved back to Grahamstown to make a home for herself and her daughter. She took a portion of Gertrude's house at 7 Worcester Street.

Was Jack Spreckley any relation? He came to South Africa in 1881 to work for four years on an ostrich farm at Fish River, 28 miles from Grahamstown. Then he went to the Transvaal and was on the Witwatersrand at the time of the famous discovery of 'banket' gold. In 1885 he joined the Bechuanaland Border Police but took his discharge the following year, when with four companions, Frank Johnson, Maurice Heany, Henry Borrow and Ted Burnett, he set out for Bulawayo to try for a concession from Lobengula, Chief of the Matabele, to prospect for gold. On the way through Khama's country a concession was obtained for the same purpose and was eventually floated as the Bechuanaland Exploration Company.

It was in 1886 that the group began negotiations with Lobengula, who at first refused permission to go to Mashonaland because in Spreckley's own words 'we should all die'. He, (Lobengula), added that when we were all dead he should receive a long letter from the white Queen (Victoria), asking where he had put the white men, and he should get into serious trouble which he wishes to avoid. When he was told that the party would carry effective medicines he was persuaded to let them go, and give them two guides, one of whom unfortunately died of malaria in spite of treatment and the other returned to Lobengula to report the incident.

There were conflicting views as to whether the party should go on to the Mazoe, as they believed had been agreed, and they consulted the famous hunter, Van Rooyen, who happened to be camped near them. He advised them to go on if they were assured that Lobengula had agreed.

"There were no survivors", an 1896 depiction of the patrol's last stand, by Allen Stewart (1865 - 1951)

23

Hugh Montague Hilton-Barber

(1872–1947)

In October 1889 a Boer commando crossed the Orange River near Naaupoort heralding the inauspicious start of the Anglo-Boer War. This was the last of the imperial wars and significantly influenced history and the careers of many great people. And this is where my grandfather, Hugh Montague Hilton- Barber, makes his small mark on history. Monty, the third son of Hilton Barber, was born at King William's Town on 15 October 1872. He first went to school in Cradock and later to St Andrew's College, Grahamstown, where he studied from 1885 to 1889. He left school when he was 17 to join his elder brother Harry on the farm. At that time Hilton had sold up in King William's Town and the family had moved to Hales Owen near Cradock. Monty was interested in starting ostrich farming but his father would have none of it, saying that sheep farming was given them a good living. Apart from that, Hilton's thoroughbred stud was occupying all his time and he was not interested in this new fad.

It was not long before Monty persuaded his father that he wanted to start farming on his own. Hilton helped him acquire a farm not far away which they called Montague. Monty still stayed at Hales Owen and rode across to his new farm every day. A week later, in October 1899 Monty volunteered from his farm at Cradock to join Major General John French's transport. He was placed in charge of a company of mule carts operating from Naaupoort to Colesberg. French commanded a division of five thousand cavalry and mounted infantry, horsemen enough to out-Boer the Boers, and he was given the task of relieving Kimberley. The General himself, with his heavy jowled face, bow legs and bull neck, was every inch a cavalry officer. He was far-sighted enough to realise that transport would be the key to success and he insisted on retaining his own cavalry division's transport outside of Roberts and Kitchener's centralised transport scheme. Monty was no stranger to transport but was frustrated by the failure of Roberts to give priority for the cavalry's baggage and his column of mule carts became trapped behind the slower-moving ox-waggons of the main infantry. The cavalry had to spend a whole day waiting on the north side of the Modder until the baggage finally arrived. The main baggage column was still marooned back at the Riet River. Delays in crossing at Waterval Drift had been so appalling that two hundred ox- wagons had to be left behind in the care of their African drivers while the rest of the column pressed forward. French, meanwhile, had personally led his cavalry at a fast gallop, sabres and lances sparkling in the sun, through a gap in the Boer defence around Kimberley and vanished into a great cloud of dust. This was the first and last time in the war that cavalry was used in this military textbook fashion. When the word came through that de Wet had ambushed the wagons at the Riet River and stampeded the cattle, Monty and his mule carts were ordered back to pick up what was left of the provisions. The Boers, of course, had long since left the scene.

There was a lot of Boer activity there and two commandos in particular, led by Bezuidenhout and Odendaal were moving about the area. Most of the farmers were Afrikaans and, if not openly supportive of the Boers, certainly did not give much sympathy to the British troops. However, Monty was well-known in the district and could count on getting some information out of them which, added to his own intimate knowledge of the surrounding country represented an important intelligence source. Hunter-Weston's company came across one of the Boer commandos at a place called Quagga's Hoek, and in the ensuing skirmish, Bezuidenhout was wounded and the Boers withdrew. (Sir Aylmer Gould Hunter-Weston was a staff officer commanding the Mounted Engineers; he was described as having "reckless courage combined with technical skill and great coolness in emergency".)

The next day Monty, knowing the Dutchman named Michau who farmed nearby, rode up to the farm house to ask whether the Boers had been seen as they had retreated in that direction. Michau was very surprised to see him and replied that the Boers were all around there and had only just left the house. He advised Monty to get away as fast as possible if he did not want to get shot. What he did not say was that the wounded Bezuidenhout had been placed on one of his (Michau's) scotch carts which was at that moment being driven down the road. Monty signalled Hunter-Weston who sent a party forward and captured the cart, wounded commandant and all. Monty advised him not to continue any further as the Boers might well attempt to recapture their leader.

However Hunter-Weston decided to push on. He and Monty rode ahead with the advance guard. When they came to a narrow pass through a dry river-bed they ran right into an ambush. The Boers had hidden themselves on a rocky hill about 150 yards away and suddenly opened fire on the men and horses as they were crowding through the narrow drift. There was pandemonium and the only thing that saved them from all being wiped out was the heavy cloud of red dust which hid everything in the valley. A number of the horses were shot and several of the men were wounded, one fatally, but most of the bullets seemed to be going high. Hunter-Weston ordered a retreat, which was instantly obeyed, he himself going out of the ambush last. Monty then commandeered a wagon from a neighbouring farm and had the wounded men taken to Cradock.

It was not long before Monty was put in charge of his own 20-strong scouting party to locate the Boers. They kept in touch with the main column by means of dispatch riders and carrier-pigeons. But the Boers were past-masters at veld-craft and many were the scouts who reported no Boers for miles only to find a laager just over the hill. Moreover, the Boer laagers could be struck with extraordinary speed. Superficially all was confusion - no tent lines, no dressing by the left or right, and no noise. But every wagon, cart and tent was laid out in the same relative position, wherever they laagered. And when a mounted Boer gave the signal, then the whole conglomeration of tents, wagons, cape-carts, horses and oxen was on the move in 10 minutes. (This was in marked contrast to the British army where the Africans were left to *inspan* 12 mules or 16 trek-oxen to harness to each wagon.) On the Boer side, everyone was trained since boyhood and lent a hand with the transport. The Boer sentries, too, were always alert - and subject to strict discipline. Sentries who slept on duty were punished by being put on ant heaps and shot if they moved.

Monty, after three weeks of hardship and toil, fell ill. The British medical officer diagnosed enteric and he was sent back to Cradock to recover. Hilton was able to convince the authorities that the sanctuary of Hales Owen and the ministrations of his mother would be more conducive to a rapid recovery than a stay at the military hospital.

To obtain a proper perspective of the war, one has to go back a further five years to the Jameson Raid. Behind this abortive attempt by Leander Starr Jameson to precipitate an uprising among the 'Uitlanders' on the Witwatersrand goldfields was the ambitious and unsubtle Cecil John Rhodes. Rhodes was obliged to resign not only as Prime Minister of the Cape Colony but also as Chairman of the Chartered Company that he and his multi-millionaire colleague, Alfred Beit, had founded to administer the new colony of Rhodesia under Crown charter. The Jameson Raid also threatened to bring down the Colonial Secretary in Lord Salisbury's Tory Cabinet, the self-made man from Birmingham, Joseph Chamberlain, equally ambitious but a lot more subtle. In fact Chamberlain owes his survival to his enemy (and Queen Victoria's grandson), Kaiser Wilhelm 11 of Germany who committed a blunder almost as colossal as Jameson's. The Kaiser sent a telegram to President Kruger congratulating him on his escape. This gave to the Raid the status of an international incident and provoked in England a storm of anti-German feeling - and invested the heretofore disgraced Jameson with an heroic aura (nothing, of course, could save Rhodes, who plunged himself with renewed energy into the business of making more money).

The Raid, ironically enough, rescued Paul Kruger, whose stock in the Transvaal had fallen so low that in the previous year he had almost lost the presidency to Commandant-General Piet Joubert, fresh from his subjugation of the troublesome native chief Mpefu. 'Krugerism' was corrupt and inefficient. Key state jobs were given away to Dutch immigrants and important monopolies, prime among them the railway and dynamite manufacture, were given away to foreigners. The fumbling old President, at a stroke, became the hero of the Raid. Jameson unwittingly united the volk, not only those of the Transvaal but also of the Orange Free State, behind Kruger.

Another consequence of the Raid was the effect it had on a brilliant young Cape Afrikaner, with a double First in Law from Cambridge, whose favourite poets were

Shelley, Shakespeare and Walt Whitman, and whose political dream was for South African unity under the British flag, a single great white nation from the Zambezi to the Cape. Jan Christiaan Smuts, outraged by Rhodes' *betrayal*, transferred his hero-worship to Kruger and became, at the age of 27, State Attorney and chief legal adviser of the Transvaal Government. Smuts was an elegant man, with his neat grey beard and his slim figure, the straightness of his posture, his calm grey-blue eyes and gentle high-pitched voice. He was generally assumed to have the qualities of a sage or a prophet and was the only colonial statesman to become an international figure in his later years.

And perhaps most significant of all, the Raid brought to South Africa a brilliant Oxford graduate with a meteoric career in the public service, a man who was to assume the mantle of imperialism, not just with a view to consolidating South Africa but for reasserting Britain's power in the greater struggle for world supremacy. But he was convinced, in his philosophy of *Big Things in Life* that in this country lay the answer to whether the Empire could be made into a reality as a federal Greater Britain, the supreme world state. He was Sir Alfred Milner, who was appointed by Joe Chamberlain as High Commissioner for South Africa and Lieutenant-Governor of Cape Colony to pick up the pieces after the Raid, following the bungling efforts of empire-building by Rhodes. Milner did not particularly like his new posting. He called Cape Town a *fourth-rate provincial town full of the most awful cads.*

Given all this, the Anglo-Boer War was entirely predictable. Without these factors, the war, in another sense, was also entirely preventable. It was surely not beyond the power of the various players to negotiate a *modus vivendi* for, on the hand, the Transvaal's claims for one million pounds' damages for the Raid (Rhodes and Beit could fork this amount out of their own pockets) and on the other, political representation for the Uitlanders in the Volksraad (Kruger was prepared to reduce the residential qualifications to seven years, partially retrospective and with a guaranteed seven seats in the 28-seat Raad).

Smuts summed it up. With an intellect equally as dazzling as Milner's, he soon realised that Milner was much more dangerous than Rhodes. He was trying to destroy the Boer state. Perhaps even more heinous, he was insulting the spirit of Afrikanerdom. Smuts harked back to Britain' annexation of the Transvaal in 1877. Although he was only a babe in arms then, the sting of imperial intervention was still in his flesh, and in that of all patriotic Afrikaners. He was familiar with Winston Churchill's statement as a political journalist in the 1880s that the Boer Republics must be *tidied up beneath the Crown. Sooner or later in a righteous cause or a picked quarrel for the sake of our Empire, for the sake of our honour, for the sake of the race, we must fight the Boers.*

In October 1899, Cecil Rhodes, who still had a great deal of political clout even though he was no longer in politics himself, arrived at his diamond capital, Kimberley, the day before the ultimatum issued by the Government of the Transvaal (under extreme provocation) to Great Britain expired. Rhodes did not believe the Boers would start the fight. He had earlier said to Milner that even if they did, their military strength *was the greatest unpricked bubble in existence.* But Milner did not make the mistake of underestimating the Boers. Rhodes, he acknowledged, *was a very great man in many ways, but judgement was hardly his strong point.* In the event, Kimberley was besieged by the Boers without a shot being fired. Rhodes issued his own ultimatum to Field Marshall Lord Roberts: *Make the relief of this town your first priority or I shall surrender to the Boers.* Roberts, who had been appointed Commander-in-Chief of the British army after General Sir Redvers Buller had been sacked for his ignominious defeat at the Battle of Colenso (in which Roberts's gallant son Freddy had been killed) was of a mind to by-pass Kimberley and take Bloemfontein.

This would wrest the initiative from the enemy. And he planned to achieve his aim by a daring strategy. Rather than using the obvious route along the rail line, he assembled an armada of ox-wagons and mule carts to strike boldly across the veld and take the Free State capital virtually by surprise, trapping the Boer raiding parties south of the Orange River and making the relief of Kimberley a simple matter. In order to carry out his plan, he and his Chief of Staff, Kitchener of Khartoum (K of K), created a general transport system in which largely untrained transport officers, hustled into mule carts and ox-waggon transport companies, were to supply all the needs of the army. This was a radical departure from the flexible system of transport which had been adopted whereby each battalion was responsible for its own transport needs. The professional transport officers prophesied disaster. They did not have long to wait before Kitchener' nick-name was changed to "K of Chaos".

His supply convoy of two hundred ox-wagons, nearly a third of the entire transport fleet, which had fallen behind the 9th Division while crossing Waterval Drift was ambushed by a Boer commando led by de Wet and most of the three thousand oxen stampeded. Their precious loads, biscuits and bully-beef, medicines and bandages, without which the army could not fight, appeared to be lost. It was thanks to Major General John French who had kept his own regimental transport out of the centralised system that disaster was averted. French's mule carts made up for part of the lost ox-wagons, some of which (without oxen) were recaptured from the Boers.

When Monty returned from his scouting duties in 1901 to resume his ostrich farming, his father, who had agreed to take over Monty's birds for the duration of the war, was now an ardent feather farmer. He had been initially opposed to the idea of ostrich farming, but with the temporary suspension of horse racing, had turned his full attention to ostriches and was astounded at the extent of the income they generated. He had the grace now to recognise the wisdom of Monty's decision to seek the best possible farm for his ostrich venture. He had sold his first farm, called Montague, and bought another, a larger one called Krantz Place, also in the Cradock district, before locating the one of his dreams near Venterstad, which he called Hilton. When Monty returned to the farm again, his father had built up his flock to several thousand. Top quality *primas* were now fetching 30 pence per lb, a fivefold increase since before the war. With this level of return, he was justified in purchasing a breeding cock, the best in the land, for over 1 000 pounds. The Cape had become far and away the greatest producer of ostrich feathers for the fashion industry. It was the most lucrative branch of farming and only slightly exceeded in export values by wool.

Hilton wanted to import Egyptian ostriches, the hardiness of which would, he felt, improve the South African breed. So he and Monty and Sidney Gilfillan, his son-in-law, set sail for Egypt in the winter of 1904. But they did not like the Egyptian birds and gave up the idea, said goodbye to the Sphinx and travelled on to England, visiting Italy and France en route. Monty took the opportunity while in London to call on Harriet Mary Silcock, who lived with her aunt Alice there. This was at the suggestion of the Silcock brothers, Boardman and Ted, who had come out to South Africa in the 1890s. They were working in Johannesburg when the Anglo-Boer War broke out. A mutual friend suggested they contact Hilton and they duly arrived at Hales Owen and offered to work for a time as learner farmers. Hilton was quite happy at this arrangement and the Silcock brothers and Monty became fast friends. So, with an introduction from her brother, Monty paid his respects to Harriet. They were immediately attracted to each other and he accompanied her to spend a weekend with her parents in Norfolk. Three weeks later they were engaged. Harriet was one of eight children, and in the custom of those days was 'given' to her aunt Alice, married to a parson in London and childless. This was a happy arrangement as Alice was able to provide a loving home environment.

Six months after her engagement to Monty, Harriet sailed to Port Elizabeth in the company of her unmarried cousin Emma, to marry her fiancé and join him on his farm. By this time, Monty had sold the farm near Cradock and was farming at Ventersdorp near the present HF Verwoerd dam. One can barely imagine the change of life-style from London to remote Karoo farm. The nearest doctor was 18 miles away - and he was a drug addict. There were no motor cars, no telephone and most of the neighbours were Afrikaans. Tiny, as she was affectionately known by family and friends, coped withal. A family friend in Johannesburg fitted out a first-aid box for her and that, plus common sense, kept them in good health. Tiny used to hire a cottage on the seafront in East London during the months of January and February every year from 1910 to 1916 when the weather on the farm was unbearably hot. She would take along one of the manager's wives or daughters to keep house, which indicates a somewhat privileged status. Frequently one of her sisters from Johannesburg would join the holiday household. Monty could not leave the farm for such a long time, and in any event he hated the sea. He used to transport the family by horse cart to the nearest station, 26 miles away, and then accompany them by train to the seaside. This was necessary as they had to change trains at Springfontein. Monty would return alone then make the journey once again to bring the family home. Monty had settled into the serious business of ostrich farming, but along with many of his contemporaries, had not the vision to foresee the clouds when they did begin to gather on the horizon. Monty, who was not entirely dependent on ostriches (he was also farming with cattle, sheep and horses) nevertheless decided to sell out and move to Grahamstown where he bought Atherstone from Thomas Hoole. Tiny was particularly pleased as the girls were due to start school there (Harold had already started at St Andrews Prep and could only return home for the June and Christmas holidays.) Another big attraction was that Atherstone was on the telephone line! Whenever anyone showed the slightest signs of illness, Tiny would phone the doctor. Her excuse was that for so many years she had had to make up her own mind as to treatment, that now she would get an expert's advice. The family's future seemed secure when Monty was able to buy the original farm Hilton on which his father was born. But then came the great depression of the early thirties which dealt the family a crushing blow. Harold, aged 16, was withdrawn from school to work on the farm. He was not in the least academic and was not unhappy to leave St Andrews College where he had been for the past four years. But it seemed to us in later years an unnecessary and harsh act of fate that deprived him of the most important years of his schooling.

Monty was obliged to sell Atherstone and acquired a smaller farm, Coldspring. His second son Tom, started a successful dairy enterprise there and Monty moved to Grahamstown for the latter years of his life, living in a small house in an unpretentious suburb, where his energetic wife Tiny seemed to be entrapped. The vast stretches of the Karoo were only memories. After Monty's death, Tiny entered into a new and amazing phase of her life that was to endure for another 40 years until her death at the age of 100. She was a wonderful caring, loving mother and companion to her ever-growing extended family, staying with her children in turn, following the grandchildren through to adult hood and then starting with the great grandchildren.

Major General John French

Sir Aylmer Gould Hunter-Weston

Kaiser Wilhelm 11

Jan Christiaan Smuts

Alfred Milner

Sir Horatio Herbert Kitchener

24

Captain Stratford St Leger

(1897–1935)

In a strange quirk of fate, **Captain Stratford St Leger**, the third son of Frederick York St Leger, was active in the same area as Monty Hilton-Barber. He recorded his experiences in written anecdotes and sketches later published in a book entitled *Mounted Infantry at War*.

It is unlikely that they ever met but this might have happened since Stratford was attached to General French's First Cavalry brigade. He commanded a mounted infantry unit assembled at the Orange River awaiting orders to advance on Kimberley to relieve the siege. At that point in the war, many foot soldiers had been mounted, better to fight the highly-mobile Boer commandos on equal terms. Stratford's unit travelled light, without tents for officers or men, each carrying on his horse 120 rounds of ammunition, emergency rations, the minimum of clothing and one day's supply of oats for the horse. After the successful relief of Kimberley, Stratford's unit went on to occupy Bloemfontein and finally Pretoria. Stratford described the ride of the relief column into Kimberley under General French as one of the most exciting experiences of the war:

> Every man in the column knew what our objective was and, stirred by the accounts of the suffering of the women and children in the besieged town, realised that what we were attempting had to be done at all costs and done quickly.
>
> The final dash for Kimberley was at 2 am on 12 February 1900. It was moonlight when they started but the moon soon disappeared and: left us to feel our way in the dark; the rumble of the gun-wheels, the shadowy forms of horsemen in one's immediate front, every now and again swaying outwards as 'ware hole!' was passed back, were the only evidences to be heard or seen of this huge column advancing. (There were three brigades of cavalry, six batteries of artillery, a mounted infantry brigade and the accompanying guides—some 5 000 men in all.) These sketches have in no sense the slightest pretensions to being a history of any phase of the A midday rest, sketch by Stratford St Leger Boer War. They are merely an attempt to depict a few of the more interesting and some of the lesser known episodes in the advance to Pretoria, as seen by a company officer who had the good fortune to serve with the Mounted Infantry attached to General French's 1st Cavalry Brigade. Histories innumerable of the war

have appeared, written both by those qualified to do so and also by others who certainly were not. Had I attempted more than these slight sketches I should have come under the latter heading. Any attempt to write a history of a war or to criticise the actions of its generals, without the writer being fully in possession of the facts and having complete access to all the information on which their orders were based, can serve no good end, and would be worthless for the purpose intended, and possibly harmful.

This volume is the outcome of a sketch book, kept up · from day to day during the war, with the idea of, perhaps, enabling me to add a few pictures, that might possibly prove of interest, to the Mounted Infantry scrap-book; at the time, however, the idea of publishing these sketches in book form never for a moment entered my head. I have endeavoured to leave out unnecessary detail that would only prove irksome to all except the students of military history, to whom this book will be of no interest. It is difficult, and I have found it impossible, in a book of reminiscences such as this, to ignore myself as completely as I should have wished. I am indebted to an old school-fellow for the account of the Siege of Kimberley; and to one who, as a Burgher of the Transvaal, fought on the Boer side, for the data on which the sketch of Life on Commando is founded. I have been enabled, through the courtesy of the proprietors of Black and White, to make use of many of my original sketches which formed the foundation for pictures in that paper.

S. E. ST LEGER. 2nd November 1903

According to our common relative, Jeremy Lawrence, he was always known as 'Ted'. He was born in 1867 in Cape Town and attended school at Tonbridge Wells in England then returned to complete a university course at Bishop's in Cape Town. He was good at sport and athletics. He married Louisa Anne, and they had a daughter Moira. In 1890 he was commissioned into the 15th Royal Irish Regiment and after serving in the Anglo-Boer war, he saw duty in the Great War, winning a DSO (1916), then CMG (1918) and CVO (1921). The Royal Irish was disbanded in 1922. In 1924 he retired with the rank of full Colonel. He died at Hove, Sussex, on 12 October 1935.

Cover: 'Mounted Infantry at War'   *'A midday rest' sketch by Stratford St Leger*

Other books by same author:

Footprints,
on the trail of those who made history in the Lowveld

Footprints,
on the trail of those who made history in Tzaneen

Footprints,
of those who made history in Haenertsburg

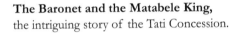

The Baronet and the Matabele King,
the intriguing story of the Tati Concession.

Hobson's Choice,
Len Hobson, the story of a remarkable man.

Kalahari Dreaming,
a whimsical anthology of poets, artists, writers and adventurers who were inspired by the desert.

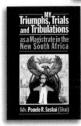

The Triumphs, Trials and Tribulations of Ponele Seshai
as a Magistrate in the new South Africa

References:

Bruwer, Dr JJ, *History of the CNA group*, Heritage Department of the City of Johannesburg 2003

Buchanan, Susan, *Burchells' Travels, the life, Art and Journeys of William John Burchell 1781-1863*
(Penguin Books, 2015)

Bulpin, TV, *Lost Trails of the Transvaal,* (Jonathan Ball, Cape Town, 1956)

Collings, John, *Gold Under Their Hooves - a History of the Johannesburg Turf Club, 1887-1987,*
(Chris van Rensburg Publications 1987)

Currey, RF, *History of St Andrew's College 1855-1955;* (Blackwell 1955)

Hockley, Harold Edward , *The Story of the British Settlers of 1820 in South Africa,*
(Juta & Co, Cape Town and Johannesburg 1973)

Joffee, Jean, *They Raced to Win, 1797-1979: A history of racing in SA,* (C Struik, Cape Town 1980)

Lister, Margaret Hermina, *Journals of Andrew Geddes Bain, Trader, Explorer, Soldier. Road Engineer and Geologist,*
Edited, with biographical sketch and footnotes (Van Riebeeck Society 1949)

Masson, Madeleine, *AVL: A Man of His Times,* (Lindlife, Cape Town 1997)

Mitford Barberton, Ivan, *The Barbers of the Peak,* (Oxford University Press, 1934)

Mitford Barberton, Ivan, *Sculptor; Ivan Mitford-Barberton,* (Howard Timmins, 1962)

Mitford Barberton, Ivan, *The Bowkers of Tharfield,* (Oxford University Press, 1952)

Mitford-Barberton, Ivan, and White, Violet, *Some Frontier Families,*
Human and Rousseau, Cape Town 1968

Pringle, Thomas *Narrative of A Residence in South Africa* 2 vols.
(Brentwood: Doppler Press 1834;1986 reprint)

Robin Richards, *Thomas Bain Lecture to the Hermanus Historical Society,* 18 April 2016

Shaw, Damian, Associate Professor of English Literature, *Thomas Pringle and the 'Hottentots',*
The Bottle Imp Issue 10, November 2011 (University of Macau, China)

Shaw, Gerald, *Early Beginnings: Cape Times 1876-1910),* (Oxford University Press 1975)

St Leger Col AY *Genealogical Chart of the Family of St Leger,* compiled by, (Cape Times 1951)

St Leger Lawrence, Jean, *Frederick York St Leger,* by his granddaughter (unpublished)

Stewart R, Warner B. Willam, John Burchell: *The multi-skilled polymath,* (S Afri J Sci. 2012. 108; 11/12)

Storrar, Patricia, *A colossus of roads,* (Murray & Roberts, Johannesburg1984)

Tabler, Edward C, *Zambezia and Matabeleland in the Seventies; The Narrative of Frederick Hugh Barber*
1875 & 1877-1878 and The Journal of Richard Frewen 1877-1878, Edited by, (Chatto & Windus 1960)

Theal, George McCall, *History of South Africa,* (Allen & Unwin 1920)

Wilson, GH, *Gone Down the Years,* (Howard Timmins, Cape Town 1943)

Wyndham, HA, *The Early History of the Thoroughbred Horse in SA,* (Oxford University Press, 1924)